COMPLEXITY = CORRUPTION

BIG TECH 5

AMAZON, APPLE, FACEBOOK, GOOGLE, MICROSOFT

A PROVOCATIVE NEW SERIES

E N L A R G E D   P R I N T   E D I T I O N

BY ACTIVIST AUTHOR DIANE FREANEY

COMPLEXITY = CORRUPTION

BIG TECH 5

AMAZON, APPLE, FACEBOOK, GOOGLE, MICROSOFT

Epilogue

Friday, November 26, 2021 6:30 AM, the day after Thanksgiving at Aunt D's Diner, on the medical mile, in Stuart, Florida.

Gloria turns on the neon signs, that blink OPEN, and unlocks the front door. I am the first to arrive, beating Chuck Rogers, Navy Seal (retired) today, something that happens rarely.

Gloria brings me iced water, coffee and places my order without asking what I want. Gloria moves slower than usual around the dining room, making sure each table is set perfectly, according to Aunt D. The dining room is decorated for Christmas with a life sized Santa Claus, a six-foot green fake tree with white lights and treasured ornaments, lighted wreaths and other signs of the season.

Gloria spent Thanksgiving eve decorating Aunt D's while her son Andrew, kitchen manager and chief cook, broke down the eight turkeys he had cooked into two hundred Thanksgiving dinners, packed by volunteers with mashed potatoes, yams, green bean casserole, stuffing and cranberry sauce for delivery to the less fortunate. Already exhausted, Gloria, husband Mike, and Andrew spent Thanksgiving day, cooking and eating and socializing with family and young grandchildren.

But I digress...

Chuck arrived about ten minutes after me, raving about his Thanksgiving meal and complaining that he ate too much. Andrew had Chuck's regular order ready - fruit salad - and Gloria put it at his place at the counter with his coffee before he even sat down. Gloria and Chuck hug, an everyday occurrence which seems to benefit them both.

Chuck's third wife passed a few years back and Aunt D's and American Legion Post 126 are his family now. Chuck calls Aunt D's every morning to report that he is either on his way or will be late and why. The dining room manager that day (Gloria, Nicole or Debi) makes sure Chuck gets a big hug before he leaves.

Why is all this important, and why is the epilogue at the beginning of this book when it is usually at the end?

Very simple, my dear Watson.

The Big Tech 5 founders all want to control our health, for profit and big bucks. The Big Tech 5 founders all use philantrocapitalism to advance their agenda. Bill Gates, and bridge partner Warren Buffet and ex-wife Melinda French Gates, initiated The Giving Pledge, ostensibly to give away all their assets during their lifetime.

In reality, the Big Tech 5 founders are using non-profit endowment accounting standards to keep control of their money and, in the process, ruin our health. MacKenzie Scott, formerly

Bezos, Laurene Powell Jobs and Melinda French Gates, former wives of Big Tech 5 founders, have signaled they want to do something different, but, in my humble opinion, their modus operandi tells a different story.

Folks who know me, can attest to my bulldogedness. I sink my teeth into a problem and do not let go until a solution emerges; or I admit that I was barking up the wrong tree, which has never happened before.

Most of Aunt D's regular crowd was MIA (missing in action) today, casualties of too much turkey and merrymaking.

Lynn and husband Bob wandered in around 7:00 am, back from their mini-vacation on Florida's west coast. Lynn has been in the employee benefits business for over forty years, owning her company since 1985. COVID made doing business exponentially more difficult and, now that the economy is getting back to normal in Florida, she is ready to sell, retire and have some fun. Lynn and Bob ate quickly and snuck out as this is a work weekend for them.

Vivian and husband Keith came sashaying in wearing their Let's Go Brandon shirts. Vivian is my unofficial fact checker and very accurate, in my humble opinion. Vivian e-mailed me a copy of the Children Health Defense newsletter, which advertised a new book, **The Real Anthony Fauci** by Robert F. Kennedy Jr.

I grew up Boston Irish Catholic in the Kennedy tradition so I felt obligated to buy and read the book. I purchased the Audible rendition - 25 hours long - and it became my bedtime listening as I was completing **Complexity = Corruption | Big Tech 5 | Microsoft**.

Kennedy reports that Bill Gates and Dr. Anthony Fauci became partners in 2000, working on vaccines, long before COVID reared its ugly head in January 2020. Gates and Fauci and Fauci's cronies made lots of moolah as long as they stayed the course and agreed with Gates/Fauci. Those that did not were better off abandoning their chosen career, retiring young and perhaps becoming a greeter at Walmart.

Kennedy reports that scientific journals started reporting promising results from studies that did not meet accepted scientific standards , pressured by Gates/Fauci to report their research as valid if they wanted to stay relevant in the scientific community.

I encourage you to read and/or listen to **The Real Anthony Fauci** by Robert F. Kennedy Jr.

Write to me at thecatlady@dianefreaney.com and let me know your thoughts. I will report out on letters I receive in The Snarky Express, my newsletter which will begin publication in January 2022.

Prologue

As a first time author, I decided to only produce and publish short form non-fiction e-books, offered for sale at $.99. It seems everyone is glued to their phones these days. These folks would love to have their libraries always available on their phones, I reasoned.

Not so, I found out, most in my audience wants paper. That was a revelation!

This is my first paperback book, a compilation of my first series of five short form non-fiction e-books, **Complexity = Corruption | Big Tech 5 (Amazon, Apple, Facebook, Google, Microsoft)**.

Patti Lucia, my writing coach, suggested early in our work together that I may want to produce a paperback compilation of my Big Tech 5 series. No, I told Patti, I only want to publish e-books. Change is happening so fast today, my books will be obsolete before I can publish a compilation.

So true. And yet my audience is telling me they want paper.

The Big Tech 5 paperback compilation is updated, reflecting my learning and changes in the political climate, locally and at the national and international level.

I do my research in bars, restaurants, diners, coffee shops and anywhere that local folks hang out in-person. Virtual hangouts like Zoom are okay one-on-one, but miss the nuances of facial expressions and mannerisms that are only apparent in person.

My first e-book **Complexity = Corruption | Big Tech 5 | Amazon** was only published on August 31, 2021. Yet so much has happened in these three short months, I am obliged to update Amazon, Apple, Facebook, and even Google and Microsoft which I just completed in the past month.

Yikes! So much additional work and so necessary!

Amazon's strong point is books. Amazon has built its foundation on its online bookstore, the place where it started - hardcover and paperback books, delivered to your home or office, now from Amazon or Amazon resellers, or delivered instantly in your Kindle or iCloud or any tablet or smart phone or Kindle Unlimited or on Audible either directly or through an Audible book club. Did I miss anything?

Some say Amazon is trying to replace the public library. To that I say, poppycock. Amazon can be the best online card catalog, freeing up librarians to do what they do best - in-person individual and group meetings with library guests to help them find the books which with teach them what they want to learn.

During COVID, I joined several online book clubs at the Blake Library, the hub of the Martin County Library System. I moved to Stuart, Florida during COVID and was grateful for any connection to my new community.

Jeanette Noe, Collections Manager, located at the Blake Library, hosted one book club. I was amazed at how many books she read and how much she knew about books in the Collection. I tried to locate and borrow a book and I was stymied. The process was so complex and difficult for a newbie like me.

I learned that the Martin County Library System, uses Libby (OverDrive). I Googled OverDrive and discovered it is owned by KKR, a gigantic private international equity fund. Therein lies the problem.

Introduction

My first paperback book, **Complexity = Corruption | Big Tech 5**, is a compilation of my first e-books series, which included an analysis of each of the big players: Amazon, Apple, Facebook, Google, Microsoft.

I believe the Big Tech 5 Founders - Bezos, Jobs, Zuckerberg, Page/Brin, Gates, meant to serve humanity, while also making a good buck for themselves.

My audience for this series is Baby Boomers (ages 55-73), who own a smart phone (68%) and Facebook (60%). (Survey Jan 8 - Feb 7, 2019, Pew Research Center). Google says Baby Boomers control 70% of all disposable income, spent mostly on experiences, not more stuff.

I am my audience: 78 years young, Silent Generation (ages 74-95), and an early adopter of technology. During 2020, I connected with my local library, the Blake Library, Martin County Library System, through a virtual book club. In my opinion, Public Libraries are the future of Education in this country.

Politicians and public figures are listed in my e-book series by name. I rely on Wikipedia and the Wall Street Journal for factual information for most of my research, which is not based on my personal experience.

Today change is happening at break neck speed. As the first book in this series, Amazon, goes to press, I am already seeing change start to happen. The Big Tech 5 CEOs are under fire from the US Congress and the Big Tech lobbyists are not able to protect them.

Ordinary folks like you and me are no longer captive customers now that pandemic lockdowns are lifting. Ordinary folks want to be outside at festivals, farmer's markets, flea markets, in restaurants and beer halls, celebrating birthdays, going on cruises, family reunions. Experiences, not stuff. High Tech, High Touch is back.

The Big Tech 5 are like one giant octopus, with tentacles invading every aspect of our lives. Octopus tentacles are mostly benign, even helpful, but there is always the fear of a venomous bite or being enveloped in a pool of black ink so dense we can no longer see.

Why is this pool of black ink so scary? It obfuscates my moral compass and is literally overwhelming.

Recently I got an E-mail from Google Inactive Account Manager Reminder telling me "3 months after your last activity, we'll notify your trusted contacts." I am 100% sure that the only place I entered the same two trusted contracts was in my Apple Watch - new to me in April 2021. I am 100% sure I have not logged into diane@rootedinvesting.com in 2021.

Complexity = Corruption | Big Tech 5 and all the titles in the series (Amazon, Apple, Facebook, Google, and Microsoft), are based on my experience and knowledge. As an activist author, I always advocate for change. My framework for change which I follow in all my e-book series is simple:

From Where I Sit | What Needs to Change?

1. Stop being Political - the Big Tech 5 are bound to offend 50% of Stakeholders (give or take) on any given issue
2. Honor Customers - Customers Pay the Bills
3. Honor Small Business Vendors
4. Honor Communities
5. Honor Public Libraries

Table of Contents

Made in America Store

Amazon Births Made in America Store

Ironically, Amazon probably birthed Made in America Store by selling cheap products from China. How, you ask?

In 2007, Mark Andol cut the ribbon on a 48,000 sq. ft. addition to the original Elma location for his General Welding & Fabricating business. Mark's motto: "You Dream It, We Build or Repair It."

Little did Mark know that the very accounts that prompted the expansion would be lost to overseas competition, currency manipulation, and the Great Recession. Two multi-million dollar accounts dropped off in the same weekend, forcing Mark to lay off half of his workforce. One of his clients claimed that he could get similar products cheaper from Florida. But it was a lie. These poor quality parts were actually manufactured in China, shipped to a port in Florida, and ended up in American warehouses in New York State and beyond.

Mark saw the crisis - laying off half his workforce - as an opportunity and after three years of planning and hard work, opened the first Made in America Store in Elma, New York, three years after the very week Mark lost the two multi-million dollar accounts. In 2012, Mark opened a Made in America Store on Amazon.com, as a third party vendor.

What's More American Than Thanksgiving?
Here's your essential list for this year's feast!

Diane Sawyer's "Made in America Series" on ABC World News put Made in America Stores on the map. His customers arrived by bus, on trips organized by senior centers, small municipalities, church groups, and other organizations dedicated to keeping seniors healthy and happy in retirement. The destination was Niagara Falls, but a side trip to purchase souvenirs made in America made sense.

Mark Andol's best customer is the best audience for my paperback books. Once my first paperback book, Complexity = Corruption | Big Tech 5 | Amazon, Apple, Facebook, Google, Microsoft is published, I plan to contact Mark Andol and to ask if he will carry my paperback books.

Mark Andol s Dream

> Mark Andol, founder and CEO of Made in America Store, allows only one item in that is not 100% made in America, in his store - his personal iPhone which he always carries.
>
> —Demick, Barbara, Los Angeles Times

Steve Jobs and Mark Andol are kindred spirits, although they never met.

Steve Jobs, the biological son of a Syrian Muslim immigrant and a German Catholic mother from Wisconsin, grew up poor. Steve learned to build beautiful things from his adoptive father, Paul Jobs, a machinist, in Paul's garage in Palo Alto, California. The Jobs home was beautiful inside, with the furniture and decor built by Paul Jobs with Steve's help.

Mark Andol, the third generation of a Greek immigrant family, grew up poor. Mark's father was an ironworker; Mark's mother built xylophone keys for Fisher Price. Mark started a metal fabricating and repair business in his father's garage in Elma, New York. His family had to repair household items. They would do without if they did not repair the items because they were poor and could not afford to purchase new.

Steve Jobs and Mark Andol were both showmen. Steve lived for the World Wide Developers Conference (WWDC) in June, and other Apple events where new hardware and software products are announced. Steve choreographed every move, tested lighting, music, every aspect of the announcement, reminding me of tech week for the Lake Worth Playhouse. When Steve was alive, all Apple contact with the public was carefully orchestrated and that practice continues today.

Although both were showmen, Mark is the polar opposite to Steve Jobs in his theatrical delivery. Mark steps on newly arrived buses to welcome visitors, stands at the door as folks enter the Made in America Store and shakes their hands, and steps on again before the bus pulls out to say, "Y'all come back."

Mark and Steve would bond over the iPhone because, in my opinion, Mark uses his iPhone exactly as Steve intended. Mark photographs and receives incoming products for placement in the brick and mortar and the online Made in America stores. Mark is always available to employees, customers, vendors, and community members who need his help, and to media outlets that want to help promote his story. Mark manages his entire business on his iPhone.

Mark estimates Apple makes $300 profit on each iPhone. Mark recommends that Apple take $100 and invest in bringing manufacturing for all iPhones sold in the United States back to the US.

Mark's original business General Welding & Fabricating had military contracts so Mark was well-versed in the Berry Amendment which requires the Department of Defense (DoD) to give preference to domestically produced and manufactured products in procurement contracts.

> AcqNotes: Contracts & Legal: Berry Amendment
>
> "The Berry Amendment (USC, Title 10, Section 2533a), requires the Department of Defense (DoD) to give preference in procurement to domestically produced, manufactured, or homegrown products, most notably food, clothing, fabrics, and specialty metals. Congress originally passed domestic source restrictions as part of the Fifth Supplemental DoD

Appropriations Act of 1941 in order to protect the domestic industrial base in the time of war. It was made permanent in 1993, then added to the United States Code in 2002."

I know some federal agencies have iPhones, but only because no technology is 100% made in America right now. Sometimes I know too much. I am aware of grift/fraud at the highest levels of DoD and I definitely don't want to spill the beans on that.

I imagine Steve Jobs recognizing immediately the opportunity to become the preferred DoD vendor for smartphones if the iPhone could be 100% made in America, using the Berry Amendment preference.

And I imagine Mark Andol as the perfect partner since Mark has experience in obtaining DoD procurement contracts. I can visualize Mark and Steve jumping up and down, hugging and clapping when they realize this great opportunity. If only Steve was still among us. I will be watching Mark Andol's next steps to make the Apple iPhone 100% Made in America.

China is A Long Drive to Work

Mark Andol seized a competitive advantage over Amazon on April 3, 2010, the grand opening of the first store in Elma, New York. From day one, Mark tells everyone who will listen, "Remember to buy American because China is a long drive to work!" And Mark gives a 10% discount to any customer who identifies as a United

States veteran, tapping into the largest and most loyal fraternity in the USA.

Made in America Store vendors increased because family-owned businesses in other states reached out to Mark and asked to be certified 100% Made in America, Mark added a wholesale department offering goods for sale to folks who wanted to set up a Made in America Store locally in their community. A collaborative model, based on the four P's that I learned at business school.

Good for People (workers, veterans, children) + Planet (local manufacturing, local delivery) + Purpose (American manufacturing) = Profit (Made in America profit).

The Made in America Store Facebook Page

I am guessing Zuck makes no AdBucks off The Made in America Store Facebook page. Mark Andol is notoriously frugal and makes full use of free advertising wherever possible, saving money to "rebuild the American dream by buying American."

I was thrilled to find that the first ever Made in America Store in Florida opened at Wellington Green Mall in Palm Beach county just in time for the holiday season.

Good for Mark!

Google Made in America Store and Get Google Ads – Really?

Google puts paid advertising before name (c) Made in America. Google's algorithms could easily be trained to go for the copyright symbol first.

I am guessing Google charges the advertiser more because the ad reaches more potential customers, but what good is it if the ad leaves the customer befuddled as to why it is seeing the ad.

Microsoft Store Sells Zero 100% Made in America Products

In fact, Made in America Store has yet to sell any electronics. Mark's favorite is his Apple iPhone and Apple has still not come around.

Global Chip Shortage

The 2020-2021 global chip shortage is causing all industries to start looking at bringing manufacturing back to the United States but that will take time. I am guessing Mark Andol and Made in America Store will be delighted to add 100% Made in America electronics to its offerings.

Made in America Store E-Mail

I look forward to receiving my weekly e-mail from Made in America Store, always spot on for the season. Now we are in the holiday season, educational toys for children, decorations for the family home and dinner table, spices and food items.

And every day 10% discount for veterans.

Invest in America First

The Big Tech 5 Founders

The Big Tech 5 founders - Bezos, Jobs, Sergey/Page started out in garages - Bezos in Seattle, Jobs and Sergey/Page in Silicon Valley, Zuckerberg in his Harvard dorm room, Bill Gates in his childhood bedroom, where he would probably still be if Mother Mary did not intervene and make him socialize.

My point is United States citizens, all $330 million of them, supported building the Internet and deserve to get something back. The Big Tech 5 founders would not have succeeded without the support of US taxpayers and yet the Big Tech 5 founders are quite okay with lobbying to bend the rules in their favor.

US citizens have sacrificed their safety net, their healthcare and their longevity to make the Internet possible. And still the Big Tech 5 lobby the US Congress and other government entities for more.

Greed - an insatiable appetite for more power, more wealth, more control - defines the Big Tech 5 founders. It is time that changed.

The Big Tech 5 Women

MacKenzie Scott, formerly Bezos, Laurene Powell Jobs, and Melinda French Gates are now physically separated from their powerful husbands by divorce or death. But are they psychologically and emotionally separated from their former husbands?

The Big Tech 5 Women are billionaires in their own right and have their own philanthrocapitalistic companies. They have signaled that they are different from their powerful husbands but their behavior tells a different story.

Still divorce and death are traumatic and takes a toll on the psyche. Recovery takes time and can be especially difficult in the public spotlight.

The Giving Pledge

The Giving Pledge was started by Bill Gates, Warren Buffet and Melinda French Gates in 2010. From the Giving Pledge website:

> "The Giving Pledge is a commitment by the world's wealthiest individuals and families to dedicate the majority of their wealth to giving back."

McKenzie Scott and Dan Jewett announced their marriage when Dan signed The Giving Pledge. Before Dan taught at Lakeside School, a private school in Seattle, Dan taught at Harriton High

School, a public school on the Philadelphia Main Line. From the Philadelphia Inquirer:

> "Of all the teachers in my life, if you had to pick one I would want to marry a billionaire to help give away her money, it would be Dan Jewett," [Josh]Verlin {AP Chemistry Class in 2006} said. "He loved the students, he loved helping us. and he loved imparting knowledge."

The concept is great but the policies and procedures of endowment accounting, which all philanthropists seem to follow, guarantee that we will just see more of the same.

The Giving Pledge is Not a New Idea

The idea behind The Giving Pledge was stolen from the merely wealthy. My friend Millie told me her biological son, Dan, knows of his parent's decision to limit his inheritance and is quite okay with the plan, even though he now has a wife and two sons. As I remember, I heard about the family's plan many years before 2010, when Bill Gates, Warren Buffet and Melinda French Gates started The Giving Pledge.

Dan grew up on upper Fifth Avenue in New York City and on the family's farm in upstate New York. Dan moved to Missoula, Montana in 1993 to attend the University of Montana (BS 1997 - Recreation Management). He went on to the University of

Wyoming, in Laramie (MA Education 2013), and (PhD Education 2019). Dan is living his dream as a leader in outdoor recreation.

Mother Millie (dressage) and Father David (croquet) are both athletes and lovers of the arts. Father David has been the board Chair/CEO, and unpaid Executive Director of the York Theatre Company in New York City since 1975.

People Helping People

The most generous people are those that have the least. The poorest folks are likely to be church goers and follow the teaching of the Bible, and tithe (give 10% of their income to the church).

I was born and baptized Roman Catholic, but was turned off by religion when I was very young when I realized that our parish priest was into money laundering. I never considered regular church attendance; weddings and funerals were enough for me. Tithing was never an issue for me.

When I lived in Portland, Oregon, I discovered the fraternal organizations - Elks, Moose, Eagles, etc. (the animals) and veterans groups. They all have a spiritual component to them which was enough organized-spirituality for me. I was recruited to join the Portland Eagles when there was a land grab going on. I stayed because I met so many kind and caring people.

The theme of all these organizations is similar: People Helping People. Members donate their time to raise money for charity when they are often living hand-to-mouth themselves. It used to be that wealthy community folks would belong to all the animal and veterans groups but that seems to have stopped, and the wealthy belong to private clubs, off-limits to homeless and sick at the bottom of society.

I would encourage the Big Tech 5 Women to become lifetime members of several of these fraternal organizations and do periodic visitations and ask them what they need.

Jeff Rifflard, my Eagles brother, is also a member of the several veterans organizations. Jeff started Diabetic Socks for Veterans, taking gifts from anyone to buy the socks and paying expenses out of his own pocket. Whenever he had $500, he would go to the Dollar Store and buy $500 worth of socks (at $1.00 a pair), print out a two page (front and back) set of instructions self-help on how to treat diabetic feet, get permission to set up a table at the local VA, and give away 3 pairs of socks and an instruction sheet to anyone who came by and asked.

Director Debra Granik Leave No Trace, hired Jeff to help the actors and the writers understand homeless Veterans with PTSD(Post Traumatic Stress Disorder). Jeff was number 3 on the credits, playing himself. Jeff recruited homeless vets and street people, who also played themselves in the movie. Jeff offered to sponsor me for membership in the local American Legion Post, but that didn't happen before I left Portland.

The Fraternal Order of Eagles was started in Seattle during the silent movie days. The orchestra went on strike which meant the movie theater went dark, because silent films would be really boring without the orchestra to create the dramatic tension.

To settle, the theater owners agreed to create a place where the men could congregate after the last show. The original FOE Lodge is still active in Seattle, convenient for MacKenzie Scott and Melinda French Gates to start their visitations and research.

I am not sure when the Women's Auxiliaries became part of the fraternal organizations. I guess the men figured out the women did all the work and needed some recognition.

As you may already suspect, I joined the Aerie, not the Auxiliary. In fact, when I moved my primary membership to the FOE Lodge 3696 in Lake Worth, Florida, I became the only current woman member of the Aerie.

The Facebook Files

I remember when Mark Zuckerberg and Priscilla Chan started the Chan Zuckerberg Initiative LLC (CZI) on December 2015. Mark was accessible on Facebook and, I think, asked for ideas how to distribute CZI funds. I told Zuck and Priscilla I thought they should invest in Internet Infrastructure, primarily in rural and poor communities, so all US citizens would have the same access to the Internet.

I envisioned everyone in America being able to communicate freely with family and friends in the US and the entire world. Certainly COVID, lockdowns and vaccines were not on my radar.

I have studied the website of the Chan Zuckerberg Initiative LLC, https://chanzuckerberg.com, and the success stories are ones I can support; yet I read **The Facebook Files** and they tell a different story.

I believe Frances Haugen, the Facebook whistleblower, and admire her courage in coming forward when she could have remained anonymous. Her accusations are backed by documents from Facebook's own files.

Priscilla and Zuck have retreated to a private enclave in Hawaii. In my opinion, changing Facebook's name to Meta is a stupid move, only initiated and supported by someone who is out of touch with reality.

Sunset Philanthrocapitalism

Philanthrocapitalism is a tragic experiment that has done the opposite of what it was billed as doing.

How to unwind the Bill and Melinda Gates Foundation? And the Chan Zuckerberg Collective LLC? And the Emerson Collective LLC? And the Rockefeller Foundation? And all the other philanthrocapitalistic organizations where rich people hide their wealth.

Simple solution.

Start with the investments.

A ten-year plan to eliminate all investments in stocks, bonds, etc. The only acceptable investments are US treasuries, bank certificates of deposits, student loans (at zero interest), affordable housing and perhaps a few others, always at zero interest rates.

You need a ten-year plan because, if you sold Microsoft and all the other stocks at once, you risk another fiasco like the 2008 global financial meltdown.

Pledges, like Warren Buffet's pledge of Berkshire Hathaway stock, would have to be paid on time in cash or the pledge cancelled.

Effective immediately all transfers to a philanthrocapitalistic organization must be in cash and have no tax consequences.

Transparency is Key

Everything must be easily accessible to the public. That should be easy for Bill Gates.

Perhaps Bill can build a computer program available to the Internal Revenue Service, the US Treasury, and the general public and offer it to the philanthrocapitalists for free, to allow the general public to follow along as the transition to community control of donated assets of the wealthy takes place.

Eliminate Non–Profit Organizations from the Tax Code

Stop issuing any new non-profit designations immediately.

Delete all twenty-eight non-profit designations from the tax code.

Notify all holders of non-profit designations that they have the option of being a benefits corporation or a membership cooperative, as defined by Martin Luther King Junior.

Small non-profits that are eligible to file a one-page report with the IRS may either report their non-profit's income and expenses on their personal income tax return (Form 1040) or convert to a membership cooperative.

The IRS Can be of Service Again

Current IRS employees who work in the Charities and Nonprofits Section will automatically be offered employment in another area of their choice at their same GSA rate and seniority.

The IRS is severely understaffed right now, which I am sure you know if you have tried to call the IRS recently.

I am sure every taxpayer in the United States of America will breathe a huge sigh of relief when this new policy is announced.

Are you listening Joe Biden?

The IRS doesn't need more money.

The IRS needs less work.

What Big Tech Needs to Change

Taking Political Positions is a Minefield

1. Fifty percent of your customers (give or take at any given time) will be offended by your political stand and, ultimately, your business will suffer.

2. Fire all lobbyists effective immediately. Ironically, the Internet and social media has created a cadre of citizens, perhaps all 330,000 US citizens, who are comfortable thinking for themselves. Stop wasting valuable money on high priced lobbyists and invest in old-fashioned customer service.

3. Open up an Office of the President/CEO and transfer all current salaried legal beagles to the Office of the President. Empower all professional staff in the Office of the President to settle any dispute for $100 or 10x the maximum value of the product in dispute. You will have fewer class action suits which will save beaucoup bucks in legal fees.

Your Customers are Pissed Because You are not Listening

1. Your customers are not stupid; stop treating your customers like they are stupid. Make a rule that all complaints to the Office of the President must have a solution satisfactory to the customer within one week if the Office of the President receives a self-addessed, snail mail letter with a real postage stamp, and two weeks if cooorespondence is by e-mail.

2. I am guessing the hackers will be bombarding the Office of the President with suspicious e-mails when they find out that the legal beagles can expedite a settlement. This is a perfect opportunity to sic your security team on the hackers and put them out of business.

Stop the Pricing Algorithms Already

1. I am a small business woman, a one-woman shop. My business is writing and publishing books. I do not have time to wade through stuff to figure out how to save two cents. One price works for me. I am even willing to pay more for superior support and on schedule delivery.

Stop Leaning on your Small Business Vendors

Running my own web site is a lot of work, but I have been burned so many times, I would rather be behind, which I am now, than trust another website designer.

Your small business vendors provide a service, give them the support that they need. Over time customers like me will trust them also.

Stick to Your Knitting; Do What You Do Best

Amazon = online bookstore

Apple = creative hardware and software

Facebook = high school and college yearbook

Google = search engine

Microsoft = business software

Jettison the other lines of business, divesting like GE, Toshiba, and Johnson & Johnson have done recently. The whole is worth more than its parts always.

Amazon – Start Playing Nice with Libraries

Libraries are the nexus of our cultural assets in the United States. Libraries are the place that recent immigrants and low income folks go to learn how to connect with the world, find a job, etc.

I just switched my publishing company to Kindle Direct Publishing (KDP) because of the services that it offered to me as a self-published author. I converted my Amazon personal account to Amazon Business because I wanted to keep my Amazon history.

Great so far! Amazon Business also makes it so much easier to work with my book designer and is saving me time.

I also want my books in public libraries and was so distressed to read this article by Geoffrey A. Fowler, "Want to borrow that e-book from the library? Sorry, Amazon won't let you," Washington Post, March 10, 2021.

> OverDrive chief executive Steve Potash told me he's had "ongoing dialogue" with Amazon Publishing. "As part of our dialogue, we communicated our willingness to innovate in an effort to support their business strategy," he said.

> "It's one thing to haggle over business — but another for Amazon to have the power to unilaterally force libraries to stay in the 20th century. It's a price we pay for letting Big Tech get so big."

> Libraries losing e-books matters because they serve us as citizens. It's easy to take for granted, but libraries are among America's great equalizers. Benjamin Franklin helped found one of America's first because he realized few individuals could afford a large enough collection to be well-informed.

> Today, the public service of libraries includes digital collections. They're a hit in urban and rural areas alike: As of 2018, about 90 percent of American libraries offered online loans. The coronavirus pandemic made digital collections only more crucial — several libraries told me e-book and audiobook checkouts surged by 40 percent or more in 2020.

You can check out an e-book or audiobook by going to your library's website and entering your library card number. Once you find a book that's available, you can download and read it on a dedicated device such as the Kindle, through the Web, or on a smartphone or tablet with an all-in-one app like Libby. When your loan is over, the digital copy disappears.

"Imagine if you were put out of work by COVID, and you want to read a book about developing your skills. You don't have the economic wherewithal to get that book yourself — but you log into the Libby app and can't find it," says Michael Blackwell, director of the rural St. Mary's County Library in Leonardtown, MD.

The Internet has, of course, given us access to a lot more information — but also made it possible to erect new walls around some of it."

"Society pays a huge price," says Michelle Jeske, city librarian at the Denver Public Library and president of the Public Library Association. "How many different platforms does a person have to subscribe to to be able to read all the things they're interested in? You used to be able to just do that at the public library."

Amazon treating digital collections differently from print is a "particularly pernicious new form of the digital divide," the American Library Association told Congress.

Another problem: Libraries can't archive for posterity what they don't have access to.

This seems like a job for MacKenzie Scott, formerly Bezos. MacKenzie Scott is an esteemed author, taught by Toni Morrison (deceased) at Princeton. MacKenzie took ten years to publish her first book through traditional publishing. Surely, MacKenzie will respect self-published authors like me and intercede with ex-husband Jeff Bezos to respect public libraries.

Apple Education – the Future of Public Education

Apple is my favorite so I reserve the two most important opportunities to change the world for good to Laurene Powell Jobs, Steve Jobs' widow, and the Emerson Collective LLC.

Google Classroom and Microsoft Team both suck. Shut them down and be done with it. In-person teaching is back, at least in Florida, so let's make the most of it and plan for the future.

Laurene home schooled the Jobs children at the huge kitchen table which dominated their space. The Jobs children are brilliant and stars in their own fields but not interested in joining Apple. I am guessing Laurene used Apple hardware and software in her children's lessons.

My hope is that Laurene will replicate her teaching methods, using Apple technology, and make Apple Education the platinum standard. I am guessing an Apple Tablet with Apple Pencil will be required for Apple Education.

Through the Emerson Collective LLC, offers Apple Education to all public schools, colleges and universities that major in teacher education at the lowest cost possible, making is easy for even the less wealthy schools to jump on board.

And encourage Apple Tablets with Pencils for all incoming students, not just those enrolled in Teacher Education, by offering deep discounts on Apple Tablets with Pencils purchased through the school. The Emerson Collective to gift each school Apple Tablets with Pencils to be offered by the school as scholarships to low income students enrolled in Teacher Education.

Newly graduated teachers will all be singing from the same song book. They can be paired with teachers with many years in the classroom, teaching the older teachers the technology, while benefiting from wisdom learned over many years.

Apple Watch – the Future of Healthcare

The best feature of my Apple Watch is Research, in my opinion. I was born with Charcot-Marie-Tooth disease, inherited from my mother. Before HIPAA, health insurance companies routinely denied claims based on pre-existing conditions; and any inherited trait was considered a pre-existing condition.

Research has an electronic copy of HIPAA-required forms before you are allowed to sign up for any Research Study. I signed up for the two I qualified for and have been diligently answering the periodic questionnaires when they are available.

The Emerson Collective LLC employs eldest son, Reed Jobs, providing his laboratory for cancer research, an excellent use of Emerson Collective LLC funds. But setting and supporting a full research laboratory over many years is extremely expensive.

However, supporting already established research laboratories through access to patients by questionnaires would move medical research ahead and bring down the cost exponentially.

My own health has improved since I purchased my Apple Watch in April 2021; one of the best investments I have ever made.

Facebook, Google and Microsoft

Dedicate 100% of philanthropy funds to make the Internet a low cost utility in the United States.

Join forces with Comcast, ATT, T-Mobile/Sprint, and Verizon to provide the same fast Internet to all areas in the United States at the lowest cost possible, using their philanthropy funds for this endeavor.

Once you have learned how to work together, tackle some of the other issues in your joint wheelhouses.

Collaboration works wonders in the Land of the Internet!

What About? What About?

What about sports?

What about games?

What about entertainment?

The list goes on, but I am tired and ready to send this book to press.

There are also many Big Tech companies not included in the Big Tech 5. To name a few: Tesla, Twitter, Roblox, etc. Some are doing great work and are becoming fierce competition for the Big Tech 5; others will crash and burn.

AMAZON

Amazon and the Land of the Internet

Amazon is a Giant in the Land of the Internet. Founded in 1994, Amazon is a Baby when compared to the Amazon River and Rainforest, which Wikipedia says are 55 million years old. Amazon, the Giant Baby, is different every day, as too many nursemaids tend to its needs.

The Early Years

Jeff and MacKenzie Bezos graduated Princeton University, in 1986 and 1994 respectively.

Jeff had careers in telecommunications (FITEL), banking (Banker's Trust), and quant hedge fund (D.E. Shaw) before meeting MacKenzie. Jeff (VP, D.E. Shaw) interviewed MacKenzie when she applied to work as a research associate to "pay the bills while working on her novels."

From MacKenzie Scott's Wikipedia page:

> In 1993, Scott and Bezos were married, and in 1994, they both left D. E. Shaw, moved to Seattle, and started Amazon. Scott was one of Amazon's first employees, and was heavily involved in Amazon's early days, working on the company's

name, business plan, accounts, and shipping early orders. She also negotiated the company's first freight contract. When Amazon began to succeed, Scott took a less involved role in the business, preferring to focus on her family and literary career.

I note with interest that Jeff Bezos 'Wikipedia page has been scrubbed clean of any mention of MacKenzie as a business partner in early Amazon days.

Amazon started as an online bookstore; curious since Jeff Bezos interest has always been to sell many products. I will make a wild ass guess that MacKenzie's interest in writing novels strongly influenced Jeff's decision to start Amazon with an online bookstore. MacKenzie was an active partner in the early years.

Jeff Bezos started planning Amazon's initial public offering (IPO) when the company was Cadabra, before Infant Amazon was even born. Early investors were warned that Amazon had 70% chance of bankruptcy. The 1997 IPO netted $54 million. Infant Amazon gobbled cash. Jeff Bezos was back to the banks and Wall Street often. I remember wondering when Amazon would go bankrupt.

MacKenzie's active participation in Amazon would soon transition to birthing, raising and educating the Bezos children. The Bezos children would have nannies to assist in their care and education. Jeff Bezos made sure soon-to-be-mother, MacKenzie, had no trouble paying the bills while working on her novels.

Infant Amazon transitioned to childhood around the time of MacKenzie's first pregnancy. Preston Bezos, the oldest son and a Leo, was born around July 31, 2000. The Bezos children and MacKenzie led private lives. The times Jeff Bezos spent at home with MacKenzie and the children were a welcome respite from his time in the limelight promoting Amazon.

MacKenzie Bezos 'first book, **The Testing of Luther Albright: A Novel**, was published in 2005, after 10 years of work. From the Acknowledgements:

> I would also like to thank all those friends and family members who rendered emotional support in the form of comfort, distraction, or childcare; my children, for countless small and priceless things; and Jeff, my best reader and best friend, whose company was itself the most frequent aid.
>
> —Bezos, MacKenzie. **The Testing of Luther Albright** (p. 246). HarperCollins e-books. Kindle Edition.

Amazon's teenage years began with the publication of **The Testing of Luther Albright: A Novel**. MacKenzie birthed two more sons and adopted a daughter from China.

The Bezos children attended Lakeside School (grades 5-12) in Seattle, where MacKenzie probably met science teacher, Dan Jewett, MacKenzie's current husband.

Enter Adulthood

Chronologically, teenagers do become adults and Amazon is no exception.

Amazon is a young adult, barely out of childhood, and ruler of all retail in our world today. First Amazon was satisfied with a piece of the pie, then several slices, now pretty much the whole pie, with only crumbs for everyone else.

At 27 years old, Amazon feels invincible, unable to fathom the dangers ahead, bringing to mind Marie Antionette, the last queen of France before the French Revolution. Marie Antionette was beheaded.

The peasants had no bread and were starving. Marie Antionette is credited with saying, "Let them eat CAKE."

Adulting is hard!

Although Jeff Bezos and the other Big Tech 5 talking heads are used to writing the rules, recent hearings in Washington, D.C., did NOT go as expected. I encourage you to read, "Congress targets tech giants Apple, Google, Amazon, and Facebook in new series of antitrust laws," by Nicole Goodkind, (**Fortune**, June 11, 2021) if you want to know more. From the article:

> Tech giants like Amazon, Facebook, and Google have spent small fortunes asserting their influence in Washington, D.C.

Executives at these companies hold a small army of lobbyists at the hip, ready to deploy at a moment's notice. They cozy up to lawmakers at expensive Silicon Valley fundraisers, and they regularly attend meetings on the Capitol and testify in the halls of Congress. But cash isn't always king: A new set of antitrust reform bills introduced to Congress Friday by a bipartisan group of lawmakers could significantly rein in big tech's power and alter their business practices.

Jeff Bezos and the other Big Tech 5 talking heads may have already started the process of change; changes that will increase shareholder returns and "improve the customer experience." I am guessing these changes will be welcomed by federal lawmakers.

Amazon Stakeholders

A Cast of Thousands

Amazon stakeholders are impossible to count so I am not going to try. Stakeholders that impact me directly are customers, communities, and vendors.

Amazon is a publicly-traded company. Shareholders in publicly traded companies are held to standards usually defined in their mission/vision statements. Amazon's 14 Leadership Principles are their mission/vision statement and define Amazon's culture.

Bezos, Jobs, Zuckerberg, Page/Brin, and Gates—the Big Tech 5—all pitch the same investors, same board members, attend the same conferences, etc. They love each other's business models and know exactly what they would change to make the others' businesses better.

The Big Tech 5 founders are ruthless control freaks. Steve Jobs is dead and, some say, still controls Apple from his grave. They are loved and feared by everyone they do business with.

Jeff Bezos, now Amazon's Executive Chairman, announced on July 5, 2021, the 27th anniversary of Amazon's incorporation, that Andy Jassy was Amazon's CEO. Jassy is seen as more soft spoken and approachable than Bezos, who can be volatile.

> "He's got just a phenomenal focus on details," said James Hamilton, an Amazon vice president who has worked with Mr. Jassy for more than a dozen years. "That relentless focus on detail is truly unique."

> —Amazon Primed Andy Jassy to Be CEO. "Can He Keep What Jeff Bezos Built?," by Aaron Tilley, Dana Mattioli and Kirsten Grind, **Wall Street Journal**, July 2, 2021

The Amazon way of leadership reminds me of ITT Corporation in the early 1970s. ITT Corporation was the fifth largest corporation in the world and I was Manager Financial Control, the highest placed woman at the company. Under scrutiny by anti-trust and beset by scandals, ITT was split into 3 separate public companies in 1995. The parts were more valuable than the whole. Shareholders made money and the egotistic men who built ITT were deflated.

At a Seattle all-hands meeting in November 2018, Bezos was asked where Amazon was headed. Bezos replied:

> "Amazon is not too big to fail," Bezos said, in a recording of the meeting that CNBC has heard. "In fact, I predict one day Amazon will fail. Amazon will go bankrupt. If you look at large companies, their lifespans tend to be 30-plus years, not a hundred-plus years."

Amazon s 14 Leadership Principles

John Rossman is a former Amazon executive who has carved out a lucrative career as a business strategist, author, and sought-after keynote speaker.

This John Rossman quote is from **Think Like Amazon: 50 ½ Ideas to Become a Digital Leader**, John Rossman, McGraw-Hill Education eBooks (2019).

> When I was at Amazon, they [Amazon's 14 Leadership Principles] were not formalized, but we talked about them every day and used them to make decisions. At some point after I left in late 2005, the leadership principles were codified. The LPs, as they are called at Amazon, play a key role in scaling Amazon by keeping a balance of speed, accountability, risk taking, and getting the right results. You need to be careful not to lean too heavily on one LP in relation to the others, and they need to be used with wisdom.

1. Customer Obsession
2. Ownership
3. Invent and Simplify
4. Are Right, a Lot
5. Learn and Be Curious
6. Hire and Develop the Best
7. Insist on the Highest Standards
8. Think Big
9. Bias for Action
10. Frugality
11. Earn Trust
12. Dive Deep
13. Have Backbone; Disagree and Commit
14. Deliver Results

Amazon Communities

Amazon Begins With A

Jeff Bezos changed the name of his online bookstore to Amazon from Cadabra, ahead of the IPO. Was it because Amazon begins with an A? Or was it because...

> "More than 30 million people of 350 different ethnic groups live in the Amazon, which are subdivided into 9 different national political systems and 3,344 formally acknowledged indigenous territories."
> —Amazon Rainforest, Wikipedia

Jeff Bezos is an engineer, a risk taker, and generally all around brilliant scientist. Jeff Bezos 'mind is built to deal with complexity.

Amazon managers are the best and the brightest that money can buy, but they lack Jeff Bezos 'brilliance, passion and drive. Amazon managers resort to what they learned in school: standardization (algorithms).

Standardization (algorithms) do not speak to me. Or to the innovators and entrepreneurs of the world.

I Am My Businesses. My Businesses Are Me.

My first memory is sitting on my father's knee, being tutored on my responsibilities in the family business. I have spent my whole life thinking about small businesses, family businesses, my own businesses.

My father was a leader in solid waste management or, as I told my friends, garbage and sewers. His research attracted the attention of MIT engineers and he was asked to join an MIT Research Committee on solid waste management.

My father ran a successful small business which supported our family and the families of his 40 employees. The MIT Research Committee expected him to work pro bono, which he did for a while, until the day he woke up and asked himself a question.

What's in it for me? His answer, "Nothing." He submitted his resignation and went back to the "boots on the ground" solid waste community, folks who did the work every day.

Amazon Is a Resource for My Small Business

Amazon Books. In January 2005, I purchased two Jim Collins books (Good to Great and Built to Last). My used bookstore was out and I didn't have the time for a trip to Barnes & Noble. The books arrived at my office in a week and I was hooked on Amazon.

Kindle. In 2010, I purchased and read on Kindle the Steig Larsson Millennium Trilogy. Once again, I was hooked. When I enrolled in the MBA in Sustainable Systems at Bainbridge Graduate Institute, I purchased all my books, including textbooks, on Kindle.

Kindle Direct Publishing (KDP). Patti Lucia, Writing Coach, recommended I consider KDP for my two book series, **Complexity = Corruption** and **Politics of Place**. I intended to publish on my favorite e-book platform, Kindle.

Amazon Prime Store Card. For every purchase made with the Amazon Prime Rewards credit card, I receive a 5% credit and free Amazon Prime. Amazon Prime comes with many perks and benefits and some funky marketing mumbo-jumbo that I frankly find confusing.

Amazon App for iPhone. The UPS Store #3631 is authorized to take Amazon returns. Owner/Operator Craig is adept at accessing the Amazon app to active Amazon Return Code and direct my refund credited to my Amazon Prime card.

1 Pete Morrello is the Irish, step dancing, sexy UPS Guy in Legally Blond at The Barn Theatre (July 15 - August 1, 2021). Pete's day job is owner/operator of two The UPS Stores in Stuart, Florida.

How Can Amazon Support My Small Businesses?

In 2010, I enrolled in the MBA in Sustainable Systems Program at Bainbridge Graduate Institute (BGI). BGI's hybrid model, weekly sessions online and a monthly intensive weekend at Islandwood, a nature preserve on Bainbridge Island, intrigued me.

BGI taught the four Ps of sustainability: People + Planet + Purpose = Profit. At Islandwood, we met in a circle every morning, checked in, shared gratitude and problems with solutions. I was the oldest student ever to graduate from BGI which gave me a different perspective from fellow classmates. My classmates worked for Amazon, Apple, Facebook, Google, Microsoft and other large corporations; few worked for small businesses.

The marriage of artificial intelligence and robotics seems to be working particularly well for order entry and warehousing operations. Robots are designed, built and programmed by computer scientists to do the heavy lifting and mindless work that cause human workers to have accidents and worker's compensation claims. Humans do the intellectual work which is more satisfying but requires a much higher skill level than folks who typically apply for order entry and warehousing operations.

On June 19, 2021, the Miami Herald reported that Florida has 500,000 job openings, as 503,000 remain out of work. Many of the 500,000 job openings pay high salaries; often workers do not have the skills required. This is especially evident to me as local restaurants that I frequent have to cut back their hours or close one day a week.

Amazon currently pays up to $20.00 an hour, with good benefits and a $1,000 hiring bonus. Amazon employees come on board for compensation and leave because they want autonomy and respect, a vicious circle for Amazon.

I go back to BGI's four P's of sustainability applied to Amazon: People + Planet + Purpose = Profit

Problem: Amazon confuses the hell out of me.

Solution: Listen to me and give me what I want and do the same for all your customers.

Amazon Delivery Day. This short form non-fiction e-book is based on my experience so let's get back what works for me.

Seldom do I actually need next day delivery. I am a one-person business. My time is scarce and I need to schedule time to receive, inventory, and put stuff away so I know where to find it next. Recently I noticed Amazon Delivery Day (Tuesday is my day) as a delivery option.

Collect all my orders for the week at a local Amazon warehouse. Put my orders in one of Amazon's famous blue plastic delivery bins for delivery on Tuesday. I will put my cardboard that needs recycling into last week's blue plastic delivery bin and leave it on my doorstep so Amazon delivery person can pick it up.

1 Nicole Sandoval aka Nikki Brown Clown waits for Amazon Delivery at her apartment in Chico, California, scoops up the packages and puts them away before Papi comes home for lunch.

My 70-plus years of business experience tells me that doing good increases profit. Raising prices without adding value usually backfires. Amazon has been raising prices by shifty use of algorithms.

Good for People (me) + Planet (recycling treads lightly on the planet) + Purpose (obsessing on customers) = Profit (Amazon's Profit)!

Amazon Warehouse System

Why does Amazon need to warehouse stuff at all? Why not license Amazon's proprietary warehouse system to Walmart, Staples and other competitors? Reengineer Amazon's proprietary warehouse system to automatically search competitor's inventories to find items Amazon's customer has ordered, have items delivered "Just In Time" to Amazon's customer's warehouse, which is now a staging area for daily deliveries. Load Amazon delivery trucks for that day's delivery. Deliver to Amazon's customers.

Amazon negotiated long-term contracts in China and other countries. Now China and other countries are questioning if those contracts are good for their citizens. Amazon is just now cautiously adding retail stores, after 27 years spent addicting customers to its online model.

Amazon Order Entry System

Brilliant Architecture! Dumb algorithms! I am a living, breathing human being; I am not an algorithm.

Successful small businesses do not behave according to algorithms. Successful small businesses survive and flourish only by relying on creativity and guts.

I pivoted 180-degrees during lockdown, closing down my 60-year-old business doing audit, accounting, bookkeeping and risk management, starting up several new businesses, including a virtual art gallery, a $100 store for collectibles and two short form non-fiction series, **Complexity = Corruption** and **Politics of Place**, which I planned to self-publish.

Amazon Attorneys, Lawyers and Lobbyists

Law schools teach every case as win/lose while I believe we are best served by finding win/win whenever possible. Mediation was offered as a potential solution but lawyers could not resist their win/lose law school training.

Law schools have begun to teach empathy which to law school graduates seems to mean be kind and caring to the opposing lawyer; and hope the losing client is not too unhappy with the result and doesn't get hurt too bad.

My father was in construction. A favorite pastime for folks who wanted to make some extra cash on the side and their lawyers was to cruise construction sites, note their location and put in a claim to insurance companies that they had sustained injury due to negligence of the contractor.

My father and his work crews were extremely safety conscious— the men took care of each other. My father visited each worksite every night at the end of the day and every morning before they began work to assure that safety procedures were adhered to. Often he took photos, in case they ended up in court.

If my father felt the person was legit, he offered to pay for a doctor's visit or some small stipend. Folks who were legit were usually grateful and accepted my father's offer. Other folks filed a claim against the insurance company, which sometimes ended up in court.

My father's informal process was his version of the Office of the President. Most successful small businesses had a process that works for their business to keep customers happy and prevent becoming a target for fraudulent claims.

Every large corporation had an Office of the President/CEO. The primary job of the of this office was to field complaints from customers, vendors, neighbors, anyone who wanted to complain. Initially, the CEO's Executive Secretary might be the "Office of the President." As Corporations grew larger, the Office of the President evolved into whole departments.

My colleague, Samantha, was an independent consultant who contracted with corporate executives to set up the Office of the President, part of corporation's quality control system, and monitor its effectiveness. As return on investment (ROI) became the only important measurement of corporate effectiveness, the

Office of the President was eliminated because its results were not easily translated into ROI.

Jeff Bezos employs an army of lawyers, both on Amazon's payroll and on retainer with outside law firms. I refer to Amazon's army of lawyers as Amazons 'legal beagles, because I see them as attentive dogs who will do anything in their power to make Jeff Bezos happy by getting the results he wants, legal or not, or in the best interest of the customers Amazon is obsessing about.

Amazons 'legal beagles write the small print that we, the users of Amazon systems, must agree to before we can do business online with Amazon. Recently, Amazons 'legal beagles changed the small print to allow we-the-users to sue instead of submitting to arbitration.

> In May, Amazon attorneys alerted plaintiffs' lawyers to the change in the retailer's terms of service. Instead of what was once 350 words on its website detailing arbitration requirements, there are now two sentences saying disputes can be brought in state or federal court near Amazon's Washington state headquarters.
> [Source: Randazzo, Sara. "Amazon Faced 75,000 Arbitration Demands. Now It Says: Fine, Sue Us," **Wall Street Journal**, June 1, 2021]

So what happens now? The arbitration legal beagles will become class action legal beagles and lawyers 'retirement plans will continue to be fully funded.

The CPA in me takes a sharp pencil to the legal beagle's process and finds reviving the Office of the President to be significantly less expensive. I do feel sorry for Amazon's legal beagles, who will be out of a job, so I transfer them to the Office of the President/CEO, and hold them accountable for avoiding lawsuits by identifying issues and concerns that are trending, implementing solutions before they become class action lawsuits.

How? Empower Amazon's legal beagles in Office of the President/CEO employees to settle all claims up to 10x the value of the product purchased, which is the subject of a complaint, or $100 for a non-product specific complaint, such as when Amazon delivery threw the package at my front door, breaking an antique window pane.

At the risk of appearing sexist, more women than men have graduated law school recently and women tend to be empathetic. Include some male legal beagles certainly, as well as a diverse and inclusive staff that understands cultural differences and can respond in a cultural appropriately manner. I predict that this will significantly reduce Amazon's costs and improve the customer experience at Amazon.com.

Amazon Customers

Rule #1 | Stop Confusing Customers

I would purchase more from Amazon except Amazon confuses the hell out of me.

I do my own research before I make a purchase. I am ready to buy when I get to Amazon.

What I Want and Don t Want from Amazon

I want a good selection of goods that are 100% made in America. Amazon does include the country of origin on most of the items I want to purchase now, a change from 2016 when I had to order and have an item delivered before I could learn that information. I promptly returned all items that were not made in America because Amazon offered free returns at the time. I guess Amazon figured out that was too expensive and changed the return policy.

Amazon Reviews

I want to opt-out of seeing reviews on my screen ever again.

> Fake Reviews and Inflated Ratings
> Are Still a Problem for Amazon.
> —**Wall Street Journal**, Nicole Nguyen, June 13, 2021

I have been burned too many times by fake ratings and inflated reviews. I would rather "take my chances" and buy because I like the pretty picture or go in person to Dollar General to examine merchandise before I buy.

Amazon Reviewer Ranking

My profile shows me as 302,409. Amazon may find that fascinating but it does nothing for me. I want all my prior reviews removed. I never want to receive another e-mail asking me to review a purchase or a popup screen telling me my review is due.

Amazon Business Account versus Amazon Personal Account

I figured out how to convert my personal Amazon account to a business account, saving all my history of purchases from Amazon. Soon I will be able to delete my Amazon personal account, simplifying my bookkeeping.

I am required to purchase a business membership with three seats for $179.00 in order to totally disconnect and delete my personal account. This is slightly higher than personal Prime of $12.99 per month, but comes with business benefits which add value for my small business

Amazon Smile

Amazon can make me smile by crediting .5% on all my Amazon purchases to my Amazon business account once a quarter. I promise I will put the money to good use in my local community.

Prime Day Deals

Amazon Prime Day deals did not tempt me this year. Last year I purchased several items, saving a few bucks. I was generally unhappy with my purchases.

For the 2021 holiday season, Amazon has fewer deals and more out of stock on advertised deals.

I think I read that sales at big box stores are up since folks are enjoying in-person shopping again. Amazon sales are down since every day prices are significantly higher and delivery dates are uncertain.

Amazon Returns

I want to be able to return anything I purchase at Amazon for any reason.

I never want to pay a return charge.

I always want a full refund.

I always want to take my Amazon returns to my local UPS Store.

Amazon Kindle

Amazon Kindle gets better every day. I have signed up for Amazon Kindle Unlimited and will be adding my own e-books to Kindle Unlimited soon.

Amazon Groceries

Ninety percent of my purchases came from Amazon during the pandemic; everything except groceries—which I will only ever purchase in person after an unhappy experience with Publix and Instacart.

Amazon Pharmacy

Amazon Pharmacy promises to get you the best price for your pharmaceutical needs even if you don't have insurance. Then I read the small print: you must have at least one prescription and Amazon will choose where your prescription is fulfilled, possibly including China. No prescription medicines for me.

Amazon Pharmacy does not offer homeopathics, vitamins and home medical tests through Amazon Pharmacy, although Amazon offers some of these items in other areas.

I would love to have one all my home medical tests in one place, along with homeopathic and vitamins prescribed by my licensed acupuncturist. I would want to give all my health care providers access to my records at Amazon Pharmacy at any time.

Self-managed healthcare is trending. Amazon is usually quick to spot trends, but it seems they missed this trend. It is not too late to pivot and get on the self-care band wagon.

Amazon Inventory

I want instructions on 8 1/2 x 11-inch sheets, sortable by category, alphabetically, in many languages and available online, downloadable to a thumb drive or print-on-demand, one page or several sheets or a complete book.

A complete inventory of household items purchased from Amazon and affiliated suppliers would become a household manual for homeowners, tenants, guests, buyers, sellers, insurance agents, mortgage bankers and any other folks I want to share it with.

This electronic household inventory would replace the paper instructions that come with most purchased items. I would purchase more items from Amazon if they made this item available. Amazon sales would increase, Amazon would do its part in controlling climate change by saving trees.

How can a paper manual save trees, you ask? As more folks rely on electronic files, fewer folks will want paper. The paper instructions that come with most items are in several languages, when only one is required by the buyer and usually in odd sizes designed to fit the package size. Paper instructions could be eliminated altogether saving time in addition to paper and ink.

Amazon Vendors

Rule #2 | Stop Bullying Vendors

The Amazon machine is so big, like a giant octopus with tentacles extending into every crevice of our lives. The Amazon machine is powerful, with an army of highly paid lobbyists in Washington, D.C. for protection.

Powerful people and powerful organizations attract bullies. Bullies pick on people they perceive as weak. Small businesses, like me, are perceived by bullies to be weak.

Small business vendors have always been fair game for bullies. My father was a small business owner long before the Internet or Amazon. The bully strategy is still the same; the Internet has just speeded up the process.

Powerful businesses, like Nike, call the shots and set up their own distribution systems. Nike will not be bullied. In fact, Nike is often the bully. The logo companies (big brands) often sell through their own websites and in person stores, and partner with other logo brands, snubbing Amazon.

During the pandemic lockdown, the big box stores (Walmart, Target, etc.) tinkered with their business models, instituting personal shoppers, curbside pickup, and local delivery. As communities opened up, some folks flocked back to in-person shopping while others continued to prefer personal shoppers, curbside pickup, and local delivery.

Some small businesses thrived during the pandemic, out of necessity. Other small businesses floundered, particularly my favorites—restaurants, cafes, entertainment venues, and locally owned and operated shops.

Families, quarantined together, needed food, shelter, and basic necessities. Promised government stimulus checks were slow in arriving. School was virtual and parents/grandparents/siblings became teacher's assistants. Small family businesses found they could not rely on Amazon for the orders they needed to survive. Small family businesses created their own order entry and delivery systems, cobbled together enough good business with resources available locally.

Amazon found itself struggling to keep up and leaned harder on employees, contractors, vendors, elected officials, etc. To Amazon's amazement, these folks pushed back. Treat us humanely, we are not robots.

Become an Amazon Seller

The Amazon website makes it sound so easy except you don't see the Amazon legal beagles 'work until you sign on the dotted line. Soon you will realize that you are working 24/7 for Amazon and shouldering all the risk.

No thank you, Amazon! I will pass this time

I have my own store on Squarespace, https://www.dianefreaney.com/art-gallery. This phenomena, of building your own store on your own website, is trending, replacing Amazon, Etsy, other sites that use the third party vendor model.

I taught myself Squarespace and built my own site. Squarespace has rules which I have read and understand. The tutorials are easy to understand. The cost is minimal and well worth the price. There are many good website builders out there. Some are free with the option to upgrade when you outgrow the free version and want more features.

Kindle Direct Publishing (KDP)

I am so excited about my newest business venture—becoming a published author on Amazon Kindle, my favorite e-book platform. I discovered Author Central, a place to organize and promote my body of work.

I recently changed my publishing company to KDP, after discovering that Amazon and Apple don't play well together. Google says that Amazon sells 67% of all e-books online and 64% of printed books online. I thought I wanted to only publish e-books but I learned that my audience wants paper books.

I am an Apple hardware geek while my book designer prefer prefers PC/Android. This dichotomy has caused some issues in our work together. I checked out KDP and found some amazing features.

For example, my Amazon business account has three seats. I transferred one to my book designer and she is able to upload and manage my e-books without obtaining my approval each time. My most recent book **Complexity = Corruption | Big Tech 5: Microsoft** uploaded in record time and came with an advertisement at the end....

> "Publish your e-book as a paperback
>
> Now that you've completed your e-book, you can use the same title information and manuscript to publish a paperback.
>
> Free online set up. KDP prints your book on demand and simply deducts printing cost from your royalties.
>
> It's easy. Use your eBook manuscript and cover to start creating your paperback book."

Got it! All my future e-books will be available as paperbacks.

Amazon Prime Store Card

Rule #3 | Eliminate Middlemen

I signed up for the Amazon Store Card because the Prime membership price increase was not in my budget. The Amazon Prime Store Card came with a free Prime membership and 5% off all Amazon purchases. Synchrony made so many mistakes on my account and made it impossible for me to correct so I stopped using the Amazon Prime Store Card and closed the account.

The benefits of Prime membership continued and I became addicted. In November 2020, an Amazon e-mail surfaced saying I would lose my Prime membership if I didn't start using my Amazon Prime Store Card.

Yikes!

I went to the Synchrony website and found it surprisingly easy to reopen my account and increase the credit line to $5,000. Amazon became my go-to place during the pandemic, especially after my local Dollar General Store closed temporarily for renovation and a deep clean.

I ordered over $5,000 last year, pretty much all my disposable income. I intended to embark on a major renovation project in my

Stuart, Florida condominium, ordering many construction materials from Amazon. I applied to increase my Amazon Prime Store Card limit to $10,000.

Synchrony denied my request because:

1. Not enough credit on revolving accounts,
2. Lack of first mortgage account information,
3. Not enough balance paid down over time on revolving accounts, and
4. Delinquent or derogatory status on accounts is too recent. Jeff Bezos is brilliant—operations, finance, etc. I am certain Bezos will find I am a good customer if he asks his algorithms. I have been an Amazon customer since 2004. I always pay my bills in full every month as soon as I receive my bill. Why would Jeff Bezos care if I had a mortgage or used revolving credit?

Perhaps Bezos thought Amazon could be another GE Credit. Bezos knows better—the anti-trust police are already trying to break up Amazon. Control credit also? That will never happen.

Bezos "got in bed" with mediocre bankers and delegated my customer status to Synchrony's incompetent bankers who are still operating in the Dark Ages, ignoring the Land of the Internet.

I choose to take Synchrony's denial as a positive. The price of construction materials is at an all-time high right now—folks are renovating their homes, commercial spaces are renovating to lure employees back to the office, restaurants are reimagining their spaces for social distancing.

Everything moves faster in the post-pandemic Land of the Internet. I am guessing that six-to-twelve months from now, the price of construction materials will plummet and my condo renovations will cost significantly less.

In the meantime, my local Dollar General has completed its renovation and deep clean, and stocks all my essentials at prices equal or below Amazon.

Recommended change: Eliminate Amazon credit cards and replace with a monthly charge:

1. Invoice all my Amazon charges once a month,
2. Charge my debit card on file on agreed upon date,
3. E-mail link to "Expense Register" for the month for download into QuickBooks with enough information to meet IRS requirements for business expense documentation.

Amazon and Wall Street

Rule # 4 | Transparency Rules

Amazon IPO – Shareholders are King

The Wall Street IPO is a theatrical production designed to get the highest possible price for the stock on the first day and thereafter. Stock prices drive everything that happens, which puts large shareholders in the driver's seat.

Amazon s Mission Statement

> "We strive to offer our customers the lowest possible prices, the best available selection, and the utmost convenience."

Amazon s Vision Statement

> "To be Earth's most customer-centric company, where customers can find and discover anything they might want to buy online."

Amazon s Core Values

Core Values 1, 2, 3, and 9 are the only ones I will discuss here. I would not be a good Amazon employee because I just find the others too confusing.

Core Value #1.   Obsess Over the Customer

I am an Amazon customer and I am uncomfortable when a retailer is obsessing over me.

From the National Institute of Mental Health:

> Obsessive-Compulsive Disorder (OCD) is a common, chronic, and long-lasting disorder in which a person has uncontrollable, reoccurring thoughts (obsessions) and/or behaviors (compulsions) that he or she feels the urge to repeat over and over.

The pandemic has spawned a huge increase in mental health issues, with few options for getting help. Amazon delivery was a necessity during the pandemic, but did it also contribute to mental health problems by allowing hoarders to feed their neurosis with just a click of a mouse.

Core Value #2.   Take Ownership of Results

Small businesses and independent contractors know they must take ownership of results or families, their own and their employees, lack food, shelter and basic necessities.

Amazon executives and managers must be reminded to think like owners because the consequences are usually minor when they don't. For example, no family vacation to Hawaii when there was no bonus.

Core Value #3.   Invent and Simplify

Amazon executives and managers seem to believe they invent and simplify. I guess that is how computer/data scientists, tenured academics, and professional lawyers and accountants see the process.

Baby Boomers and older, not so much. Imagine how much Amazon could increase sales if they decided to tap into this market. Baby Boomers control 70% of disposable income.

Core Value #9. Practice Frugality

. . . is one Leadership Core Value I want to explore more. Andy Jassy's salary of $175,000 is the highest in the company. One of the first things Jassy did when he became CEO was remind folks to book coach when traveling for Amazon.

So how do Amazon executives become millionaires, even billionaires, when the top salary in the company is $175,000? Why bonuses and stock options, of course. Which is why Amazon has so many lifers like Andy Jassy. Stock options and even bonuses can be paid over time, tying folks to Amazon for life. Amazon has created the Internet version of the company store.

Amazon and Philanthropy

Rule # 4 | Transparency Rules

Ironically, Jeff Bezos is the only Big Tech 5 Founder, who is also a billionaire than has not signed The Giving Pledge.

I am guessing that MacKenzie Scott, formerly Bezos, Dan Jewett and Melinda French Gates are friends since the Bezos children and the Gates children are Lakeside students and alums.

I am watching the drama unfold as Melinda and Bill Gates divorce. Melinda is using MacKenzie's legal team. Melinda and Bill have announced they will co-chair the Bill and Melinda Gates Foundation, but even that seems questionable as the divorce is finalized.

The talking heads of the Big Tech 5 are all men. My money is on the Big Tech 5 women to take charge, as MacKenzie Scott and Melinda French Gates are doing, and change the world

I spent more than 20 years working as Chief Financial and Investment Officer at foundations and non-profit organizations, and have strong feelings about good and evil in philanthropy. Look for future e-books in my book series **Complexity = Corruption** and **Politics of Place**.

Bezos Day One Fund

> "The Bezos Day One Fund, a $2 billion philanthropic fund launched in 2018 by Amazon.com founder and CEO Jeff Bezos and his then-wife, MacKenzie Scott, has announced grants totaling $105.9 million in support of efforts to assist families experiencing homelessness."
> —Source: **Philanthropy News**, December 10, 2020

The Bezos Day One Fund is the exact opposite of The Giving Pledge gifts of MacKenzie Scott. MacKenzie Scott and Dan Jewett are giving away MacKenzie Scott's personal wealth.

Bezos Day One Fund is a private foundation and must, by law, give away a minimum of 5% of principal each year and file IRS Form 990-PF. Bezos Day One Fund website lists grants made for 2018, 2019, and 2020 but does not include Form 990-PF. The purpose of IRS rules is to prevent hoarding.

The biggest hoarders: Harvard, Yale, the University of Texas, Stanford, and Princeton. **New York Times** Op Ed Opinion Piece, Stop Universities From Hoarding Money, by Victor Fleischer, gives a comprehensive review of the problems hoarding creates.

Amazon Smile

Amazon Smile sounds like a great program, .5% donated to the charity of my choice, except in order to get credit for

AmazonSmile, I have to log into the AmazonSmile website and learn a whole new process for purchasing stuff on Amazon.

My charity, the Lake Worth Playhouse, has a credit of $.68 based on my purchases this year. No wonder AmazonSmile is the laughing stock of the non-profit world. AmazonSmile would generate $25.00 on my purchases last year of $5,000. That is not even worth my time to read the small print or learn how to operate the AmazonSmile website.

In my opinion, Amazon executives need to circle back to leadership principle #3 Invent and Simplify, and eliminate the AmazonSmile department. Message all customers:

> Effective October 1, 2021, AmazonSmile will issue a credit of .5% of your purchases delivered to a verified USA address for the quarter to your account or to the account of a community organization that you designate. The credit will be applied automatically to your next purchase or the next purchase of your designee.

Philanthropy is a big part of the income inequality problem in this country, in my humble opinion, and the Big Tech 5 have made income inequality exponentially worse.

I am about simple. I know why Amazon did what they did. It doesn't work for me.

APPLE

The Hero s Journey

Do that thing that fills you with the most joy and do it no matter what. That is the starting place for a real life hero's journey.

We will use a well-documented, easy example - Steve Jobs. Steve Jobs went on the same journey as the Holy Grail Knights. He followed his bliss into the forest of Silicon Valley. There was no path, he blazed his own. As he traveled, miracles of coincidences manifested, as well as epic disasters that he had to overcome. Finally, he found the Grail and returned to share it with all of us. Thank God, because I don't know what I would do without this thing [holds up iPhone]. If you have a touch screen smart phone, you know what I am talking about.

—What is the Hero's Journey?, Pat Soloman at TEDxRockCreekPark (May 11, 2013)

The Hero's Journey was unfamiliar to me so I Googled it. The top choices were TEDx Talks by men with careers in the film industry. Aha! The Star Wars connection: George Lucas credited Joseph Campbell's work on **The Hero's Journey** as influencing Star Wars.

69

I was much too serious in my teens and twenties to spend much time on Hollywood movies. I devoured boring business books so I could join the family business. And when I became interested in film later in life, it was independent film, primarily documentaries.

Steve s Reality Distortion Field

I was curious to know more about Steve's Reality Distortion Field (RDF) and why it was such a big deal at Apple. I thought about my own life and the times that I buried feelings because they were too painful, sort of like hiding from myself. So why is Steve Jobs Reality Distortion Field so important to his story?

Steve Jobs, by Walter Isaacson, (Simon and Shuster. 2011), a biography authorized by Steve Jobs, contains many examples of Steve's Reality Distortion Field and how it impacted folks around him, not just at Apple but in the community.

The first page of Isaacson's book:

> "The people who are crazy enough to think they can change
> the world are the ones who do."
> —Apple's "Think Different" commercial, 1997.

Steve's inner circle included mostly strong personalities, other folks moved on. The old cliché, "If you can't stand the heat, get out of the kitchen."

My favorite story from Isaacson:

> One day Jobs came into the cubicle of Larry Kenyon, an engineer who was working on the Macintosh operating system, and complained that it was taking too long to boot up. Kenyon started to explain, but Jobs cut him off. "If it could save a person's life, would you find a way to shave ten seconds off the boot time?" he asked. Kenyon allowed that he probably could. Jobs went to a whiteboard and showed that if there were five million people using the Mac, and it took ten seconds extra to turn it on every day, that added up to three hundred million or so hours per year that people would save, which was the equivalent of at least one hundred lifetimes saved per year.
>
> "Larry was suitably impressed, and a few weeks later he came back and it booted up twenty-eight seconds faster," Atkinson recalled. "Steve had a way of motivating by looking at the bigger picture."
>
> —Isaacson, Walter. **Steve Jobs**. Simon & Schuster, 2011.

Another good story:

Beginning in 1981, the Mac Team gave an award to the person who did the best job standing up to Steve Jobs. Joanna Hoffman won the award in 1981 and again 1982. Debi Coleman won in 1983. I find it interesting that women won the first three years of the award.

Steve s Biography

Why is Walter Isaacson's biography of Steve Jobs important? Isaacson made Steve, his families and the folks at Apple come alive. Steve agreed not to meddle in Isaacson's interview process, not to put any topic or person off limits, and he kept his word.

> Laurene Jobs also encouraged Isaacson, "There are parts of his life and personality that are extremely messy, and that's the truth," she told me early on. "You shouldn't whitewash it. He's good at spin, but he also has a remarkable story, and I'd like to see that it's all told truthfully."

Steve did not meddle, in fact he did not even read the entire book. Interestingly, Steve saw an early version of the cover art and hated it so much he asked to have input and Isaacson agreed. Visually, this is how Steve Jobs wants to be remembered.

I encourage you to read Isaacson's book, if you want to learn the full story of Steve Jobs and Apple.

My Favorite Big Tech 5

Apple and Steve Jobs are my favorite of the Big Tech 5.

Here's why...

Let me list some ways Apple and Steve Jobs are different from the other four Big Tech 5 and their Founders.

First, Apple:

—Apple is the least political of the Big Tech 5
—Apple is hardware first; software and services second
—Apple is creative artist first; business second
—Apple seeks perfection; shuns good enough

1 The cover of Walter Isaacson's book **Steve Jobs**. Simon & Schuster (2011)

Second, Steve Jobs:

—Steve's birth parents were wealthy
—Steve was adopted
—Steve grew up poor
—Steve's adoptive father, a machinist, taught him to make
  beautiful things with his hands
—Steve did not attend an Ivy League School

The Jobs Families

Steve Jobs had many families, something that is common today, but unusual when I grew up and "Leave it to Beaver" families were the norm, i.e. a white picket fence, 2.2 kids and a dog, stay-at-home mom and a dad that went to the office every day and brought home the bacon.

Married Life (1991–2011)

Steve and Laurene met at Stanford Business School when Steve gave a lecture. Laurene commandeered a reserve seat and Steve Jobs sat next to her. She told him she had won a raffle and he got to take her to dinner. They went to dinner and stayed together until his death.

Walter Isaacson describes Laurene as the perfect match for Steve Jobs:

> Smart, yet unpretentious. Tough enough to stand up to him, yet Zen-like enough to rise above turmoil. Well-educated and independent, yet ready to make accommodations for him and a family. Down-to-earth, but with a touch of the ethereal. Savvy enough to know how to manage him, but secure enough to not always need to.

In 1991, Steve and Laurene married in a ceremony conducted by Steve's longtime Sōtō Zen teacher, Kobun Chino, at Ahwahnee Lodge in Yosemite National Park. Reed Paul Jobs, their only son, was born three months after their wedding; daughter Erin Sienna arrived in 1995; and daughter Eve in 1998.

In 1990, Laurene co-founded Terravera, a natural foods company that sold to retailers throughout Northern California. She backed off from Terravera, preferring to spend her time preparing vegan meals for Steve and catering to his sometimes crazy food fetishes, and raising and tutoring their children. Little is known about Steve Jobs' children because they were not allowed to be on social media. This seems to be a common theme for children of tech families in Silicon Valley.

In 2004, Powell Jobs founded the Emerson Collective, a private limited liability company that supports education and immigration reform, social justice, media, and journalism, and conservation through partnerships, grants, and investments. Reed Jobs is employed by the Emerson Collective as a cancer researcher.

Partnership Family (1972–1977)

Chrisann Brennan and Steve Jobs met and began dating when they were in high school. They continued dating after Steve went to Reed College in Portland, Oregon, until Steve decided to audit classes so Paul Jobs, his adoptive father, did not have to pay tuition, room and board. Chrisann wrote a book, **The Bite in the Apple: A Memoir of My Life with Steve Jobs**.

Chrisann and Steve's daughter Lisa Brennan Jobs was born May 17, 1978 at the All in One Farm. Lisa Brennan-Jobs wrote **Small Fry: A Memoir**.

Reed Family and Roommates

Steve found a crazy family in his fellow students at Reed College. They moved in together often and sometimes Steve moved back in with his adoptive parents Paul and Clara Jobs. Abandonment became a theme in Steve's life. He couldn't stand to be alone, but when he was with people he abused them and treated them like shit.

Adoptive Family

Paul Rheinhold Jobs and Clara Jobs were a hardworking, working class family who did everything within their means for their adoptive son and daughter. Steve was particularly close to Paul Jobs, Clara not so much. Clara was afraid to love Steve for the first year because she was afraid he would be taken from them. Then the adoption was final and Steve entered the terrible twos and she wasn't sure she even liked him.

> "Knowing I was adopted may have made me feel more independent, but I have never felt abandoned. I've always felt special. My parents made me feel special." He would later bristle whenever anyone referred to Paul and Clara Jobs as

his 'adoptive' parents or implied that they were not his 'real' parents. "They were my parents 1,000%," he said.
—Isaacson, Walter. **Steve Jobs**. Simon & Schuster, 2011.

Birth Family

When speaking about his biological parents, on the other hand, he was curt:

> "They were my sperm and egg bank. That's not harsh, it's just the way it was, a sperm bank thing, nothing more."
> —Source: Isaacson, Walter. **Steve Jobs**. Simon & Schuster, 2011.

Apple Devices

Apple II and VisiCalc

In the summer of 1980, I was privileged to attend the Corporate Finance Executive Education Program at the Harvard Business School (HBS). I walked into my room in the Advanced Management Program dorm and was freaked out by the Apple II computer sitting on my desk. I had an Apple II computer just like it sitting on my desk back at Safeguard Business System. I thought, "Oh my God, it followed me here."

The Safeguard Research Team had given me the Apple II when they moved on to Novell in Provo, Utah. The Apple II came with instructions that I didn't understand. I periodically turned it on and thought, "I can do this!" But I could only get it to beep at me.

The first evening at dinner, we met our fellow students, seventy-eight white men, a black guy and me, the only woman. The program director, Samuel Hayes, investment banking professor at the HBS, gave a brief speech after dinner telling us what to expect: Harvard case studies, three a day, with one case study using VisiCalc. The next morning, Dan Bricklin, HBS MBA and co-creator of VisiCalc, would teach us VisiCalc. Dan, with the help of fellow MIT alum Bob Frankton, wrote VisiCalc for his MBA thesis.

The next morning, we met in the lobby of our dorm and walked over together to our classroom for the session, a tiered-seating room, with presentation space at the bottom. An Apple II sat in the middle of the presentation space, with white boards on wheels on either side. At exactly 8:00 am, the presenters entered stage left, Sam, clean shaven in a business suit and Dan, with a full beard, a plaid shirt and jeans.

Sam introduced Dan and the Technical Assistants (TA). Sam said that each team room had an Apple II with VisiCalc. After Dan's presentation, student teams would meet with a TA in the team room. The TA would give us a hands-on look at the Apple II, review Dan's presentation, and answer our questions. I learned to love Apple and spreadsheets.

Back at the office, Pete Musser said Safeguard was negotiating to buy a payroll company to beef up Safeguard's product offerings. Pete needed a financial presentation for the board meeting. He gave me the basic facts and assumptions, which I fed into VisiCalc. I did several iterations, each time changing an assumption, until the financial model matched the vision that Pete wanted to present to the board.

The board approved Pete's plan to purchase the payroll company and complimented him on the excellent presentation. Pete said that I had prepared the financials and, by using an Apple II and VisiCalc, we were able to do several iterations until the plan made sense. Suddenly, I had all ten board members in my tiny office asking me to demonstrate VisiCalc.

Yikes!

The impromptu meeting in my office did not go well. My Apple II had 48K RAM which allowed VisiCalc to crunch accurate numbers very, very slowly. I lacked Pete Musser's charisma and the numbers were just as boring on the Apple II's green and black screen as they were on paper.

Dan Bricklin, in his TedXBeachStreet talk, quoted Steve Jobs telling an interviewer, "VisiCalc propelled the success of Apple more than any other single event. If VisiCalc had been written for some other computer, you would be interviewing someone else right now."

Steve Jobs must have found traditional spreadsheets boring also and when the Apple spreadsheet, Numbers, was released in 2007, it had all the razzle dazzle that Steve Jobs and Apple are famous for.

My iPhones

Sprint sent me a large postcard, notifying me that I was entitled to a new phone. I passed the Apple Store on the second floor of the Palm Beach Gardens Mall next to Bloomingdale's, on my way to Sprint. I admired the iPhones and said to myself, "I want an iPhone."

My niece and I signed up for a Sprint Family Plan, when I was visiting her in Southern California. Sprint advertised a great promotion and we were first in line when the store opened. The Sprint salesman was alone and the setup did not go well. A Sprint supervisor arrived after a while and completed the setup. We were happy enough with our new phones, but happy with the cost savings.

The Palm Beach Gardens Mall Sprint salesman told me that we had to go to the same store in Los Angeles together in order to get new phones. He brought out a copy of our contract and pointed to the fine print.

"I do not live in Los Angeles," I said. "Sprint knows that because Sprint sends the Sprint Family Plan bill to my Florida address and I mail Sprint a check." The Sprint salesman would not budge. I had a hissy fit and stormed out of Sprint and back to Apple.

I checked out the iPhones and decided which one I wanted, while waiting for a salesman. ATT and Apple had an exclusive contract to sell iPhones and porting numbers had just become common. I could keep my number if I signed up with ATT. I signed ATT's small print contract.

The salesman set up my new iPhone and gave a brief overview of how it worked. I bought a paperback book that gave an overview of the iPhone features. I spent the rest of the weekend at home reading the book and learning how to use my new iPhone.

In December 2016, I bought myself an iPhone 7 Plus for Christmas at the Apple Store in Portland, Oregon. The iPhone 7 Plus was a powerful tool, so much more than a phone. During the pandemic, my phone had some hiccups. I started taking more photos and downloading files, and I was running out of space.

I rediscovered the **Wall Street Journal** and was pleasantly surprised at the creativity and the quality of the reporting. I decided to purchase the iPhone 12 Pro Max, based on Joanna Stern's article , "iPhone 12 Pro Max Review: Bulkiest iPhone Bumps Up Camera and Battery," (**Wall Street Journal**, November 9, 2020). Joanna's five-minute video focusing on the camera sold me. Joanna's only negative was how big the iPhone Pro Max was. I got out my ruler and measured my iPhone 7 Plus in its case and found it to be about the same size.

I love the camera and take photos often. I took my own author's photo, my first selfie, at Carson's Tavern.

I eat out every day in some of the finest restaurants, cafes, diners and bars in Stuart, Florida, and I post photos of my meals on Facebook.

I always avoided apps; now I am finding some useful. I have downloaded and paid for some apps that just did not work as expected. I called Apple, the customer care representative listened, helped me uninstall the app and got me my money back.

I get my news from the Wall Street Journal app, and keep a supply of books on Kindle. I can find my files on iCloud and Dropbox. I have begun using Day One, a daily diary where I store my food photos and some daily notes. I am delighted to be able to do all this on my phone.

I am not the least bit tempted to consider purchasing the new iPhone. I hope the iPhone 12 Pro Max will last me for at least the next five years.

Tim Cook and Craig Federighi have done a good job shepherding Apple according to Steve Jobs 'vision, but can they step up to the plate and take Apple to the next level? Steve was the star, brilliant—with an IQ higher than Einstein—and mercurial, behaving like a two year old brat at times.

Steve's children are brilliant and have carved out their own careers, out of the limelight, with no interest in a career at Apple. Steve's wife, Laurene Powell Jobs was a stay-at-home mom, taking care of Steve and his children during their time together, and for several years after Steve's death. Recently, Laurene Powell Jobs has stepped into the limelight politically, something that Apple successfully avoided while Steve was alive.

My MacMini

It would be 38 years before I had another Apple desktop, after the Apple II. I was fascinated by VisiCalc, but lusted after more computer power, 48K didn't support much number crunching, and Apple was slow to introduce a more powerful replacement for the Apple II.

In November 1980, Pete Musser, CEO of Safeguard Scientifics, provided $2 million in seed funding to Novell Data Systems. Pete believed that Novell could help automate the manual One-Write Systems of Safeguard Business Systems. Novell NetWare, a multi-platform network operating system was one of Novell's best products. The small business computers, computer terminals, and other peripherals that co-founders George Canova and Jack Davis intended to manufacture and market were inferior to other PC DOS-based products.

3 My MacMini with Benq Monitor on my desk.

By the first quarter of 1982, Novell's costs were out of control and prospects for future hardware sales were dim. Novell's poor performance negatively impacted Safeguard Scientifics ⋅stock price. Pete sent Jack Messman to Utah to fire Canova and Davis, and take over as president. Jack cut expenses to the bone and, as I recall the story, was just about to turn the lights out forever when the first big order for its network operating system came in. Novell transitioned from a hardware to a software company.

Ray Noorda and Jack Messman connected at COMDEX - Las Vegas (November 1982). Ray Noorda, a former General Electric executive, with a reputation as a turn-around expert, became president of a newly reorganized Novell, Inc. on April 1, 1983. At its high point, NetWare had a 63% share of the market for network operating systems, and by the early 1990s there were over half a million NetWare-based networks installed worldwide encompassing more than 50 million users.

From Novell's Wikipedia page:

> As author James Causey would later write, "NetWare deserves the lion's share of the credit for elevating PC-based local area networks from being cute toys to providing powerful, reliable, and serious network services."

How did this affect me? Safeguard's experiment with Apple II and VisiCalc was over and our office settled on PCs. Dell had the best prices so we ordered in bulk and everyone had a PC on their desk, loaded with Lotus 1-2-3. I spent most of my time building financials models for acquisitions, new product lines, and public reporting. I was able to attract an amazing assistant treasurer and together we built a cash management system, which one of our bankers told us was the best he had ever seen.

My firsthand experience makes me especially critical of algorithms and artificial intelligence today. I know what can go wrong. I probably made all the same mistakes myself, until I applied the old accounting rule: the debits must equal the credits.

Bob, a financial systems coder and analyst, recently retired, said he knows exactly why systems fail. The number one rule of coding is you can add code but you can never eliminate a line of code. The "kids" who are doing coding never learned. They think, I don't need that and it is gone, and the system fails.

Apple and VisiCalc jumpstarted a stalled career for me and I am grateful. As I embark on a new career as an author, it is time to come back to Apple. I rediscovered the **Wall Street Journal** and marvel at how much it has changed for the better since the paper copy I read every morning when I was in my twenties.

I love Joanna Stern and her creative and insightful Apple Reviews. So, when my iPhone and MacBook Pro laptop started having problems, I decided to follow her recommendations.

I read Joanna's reviews of the M-1 chip and decided on a MacMini desktop with an M1. The MacMini is tiny, roughly 8 inches square x 2 inches high. So much nicer that the big Dell desktops. I watched the instruction video and was able to set up the MacMini myself—

all except loading classical Word and Excel, which was a nightmare that I discuss further under Numbers.

Apple software seems to have taken another giant step forward. My MacMini told me my Apple Watch was unable to unlock my MacMini and I would have to log in. Beyond freaky!

Apple Laptops

My MacBook Pro served me well for many years. I began having problems connecting to the Internet, I took it to the Palm Beach Mac Service Store in West Palm Beach. The tech ran diagnostics, told me it was a known issue and they would replace the motherboard for free even though the service contract had lapsed. I had to leave it for two days but it was worth it to have essentially a brand new computer.

My MacBook Pro served me well while I researched, planned and budgeted to upgrade all my technology. I am aware that Apple is always the high cost option and still the cost of new Apple equipment is substantially less for more power and bells and whistles than the Apple laptops and iPhone I was replacing when they were new.

My MacBook Air

I purchased a MacBook Air as a student at Bainbridge Graduate Institute (BGI). I had to schlep myself and my books on Amtrak to Seattle, make my way to the Bainbridge Island ferry from the Amtrak station, and then from the ferry to Islandwood. The MacBook Air was lightweight and fit easily in an over-the-shoulder bag with an iPad Mini, which I used exclusively for Kindle books and textbooks. I was using my MacBook Pro as a desktop and, since I hadn't quite figured out cloud storage yet, I didn't want to risk losing it or having it stolen.

My MacBook Air served me well during school. After graduation, I loaned it to friends and neighbors in Portland. Most of my Portland friends were artists and had learned to run their businesses, actually their lives, on their phones. Finally, I shipped it to my niece after her desktop died, with the hope that she could use it for her writing career. It had not been used for so long it would barely turn on. The Apple Store was able to diagnose the problem and install a new battery and, last I heard, it is working just fine.

4 My MacBook Air next to easy chair in my bedroom.

I got hooked on online theater during the pandemic. I would sit in my easy chair next to my bed with my MacBook Pro on my lap and watch readings at Palm Beach Dramaworks or plays at the Irish Repertory Theater. So easy—no long drive to the theatre, trying to find parking, and driving back home late at night. I put snacks and a glass of wine on the small chest next to my bed and settled down for an enchanted evening. Sometimes my laptop would sound like it was making soup. It would get hot and noisy and I had the sense that the actors could hear and were annoyed. Of course, the actors could not hear, it was my imagination.

I watched Joanna Stern's review of the M1 MacBook Air and put a MacBook Air in my 2021 budget. The MacBook Air syncs automatically with my iPhone and Apple Watch. The Apple Watch opens the MacBook Air, which was a little freaky in the beginning, but I have gotten used to it. However, the MacBook Air will lose internet connection for no apparent reason, a Comcast problem I believe, but I have no time to troubleshoot.

5 A close up of my MacBook Air, working on my writing in Scrivener.

The MacBook Air has limited ports so I recommend purchasing a 4-in-1 USB port. I also find Apple's Trackpad annoying and prefer a wired mouse, available online from other vendors.

Apple iPad Maxi and iPad Mini

Just after the first iPad Maxi was released, I remember seeing a story about a woman who had macular degeneration and could now read books on the iPad her daughter gave her for Christmas. Brilliant, I thought! I have several friends with macular degeneration who loved to read. Now they can read again.

I have the Kindle app loaded on my iPhone and my MacBook Air so I always have my books with me if I am waiting to meet a friend, on public transportation, or eating alone in a restaurant.

I respect that some folks prefer paper books, just not my cup of tea. My old eyes are so happy to see a bright screen with large letters. I am thrilled with all the improvements over the years. I have never owned an actual Kindle, but the Kindle app works just fine.

iPad, Pencil and Keyboard

I had some money left in my budget at the end of December so I couldn't resist buying an iPad mini, with a Pencil and Keyboard. Almost immediately I knew it was a mistake. The Pencil was a foreign object to me and I did not have the time to devote to learning how to use it.

My friend's grandson had been complaining that Roblox, a game he plays online with his cousins and friends from school, did not load correctly on his current iPad. I asked my friend if her grandson would like the Apple iPad with Pencil and Keyboard. Her grandson wanted it for his artwork and the comic strips he is creating with some school buddies, as well as Roblox.

My Apple Watch

I was watching Joe of Tek Medics diagnose Comcast issues when Mickey Mouse on his watch came alive, tapped his toes and said, "Good Afternoon! It's two o'clock." I said, "Where did you get that? I want one."

7 Minnie Mouse Face on my Apple Watch.

Joe enthusiastically launched into a demonstration of his Apple watch, focusing almost entirely on how he used features like the ECG to manage his own health. We went online to the Apple Store and ordered an Apple Sports Watch with a white band. My Apple Watch was scheduled to arrive in three weeks, except that it didn't. It arrived in three days.

Joe promised to set up my Apple Watch, but had a string of emergencies so I tried to set it myself. Big mistake! I got my Apple Watch to tell time but not much else.

I asked Craig at Schramm Physical Therapy to help me set up my twice weekly PT routine. Craig did a factory reset and had my routine online in 10 minutes. It took a couple of PT sessions, but now I am meeting new challenges every day.

I always knew I had breathing problems, a fact I attribute to Charcot-Marie-Tooth disease, a genetic disorder that I inherited from my mother. My Apple Watch measures blood oxygen levels automatically at random times whenever I am wearing my watch, highlighting my breathing problems in a whole new way.

Healthy blood oxygen levels range between 95 and 100 percent. My blood oxygen level is between 78 and 100 percent since I began tracking on my Apple Watch, and with a monthly average between 81 and 93 percent. A **Healthline** article reports "...people with chronic health conditions many need to monitor their blood oxygen level. This includes asthma, heart disease, and chronic obstructive pulmonary disease (COPD)."

Over the years, I remember complaining to my doctor at my annual physical about extreme fatigue, but I have no recollection of my blood oxygen level being tested. I was careful to keep my Charcot-Marie-Tooth secret for fear of being denied insurance coverage because of my pre-existing condition. In the olden days, before the Affordable Care Act, insurance companies used every excuse to deny coverage. The end result, in my opinion, is that we the public got substandard medical care even when we had insurance.

My Apple Watch partners with my iPhone which makes me happy since my old eyes find it difficult to assess my health indicators on the small face of my Apple Watch.

Apple Apps

Apple App Store

I always avoided apps; now I am finding some useful. I have downloaded and paid for some apps that just did not work as expected. I called Apple, the customer care representative listened, helped me uninstall the app and get my money back.

I get my news from the **Wall Street Journal** app and keep a supply of books on the Kindle app. I can find my files on iCloud and Dropbox. I have begun using Day One, a daily diary where I store my food photos and some daily notes on my work as an author. I am delighted to be able to do all this on my iPhone.

My complaints about App Store Apps: they come with one to three months free and then a hefty monthly charge. The learning curve is steep and the value of the app to me is marginal so my 3 months lapses before I even look at the app.

I find the sleep apps on the Apple Watch particularly annoying. The only way for me to track sleep on my Apple Watch is with an app and the apps are expensive and hard to use. How do I delete the app advertisement on my Apple Watch?

Mail

I was determined to get as far away from Google as possible after my computer shut down from e-mail spam and it took me three days to recover.

I set up diane.freaney@icloud.com and purchased several private email accounts through NameCheap, my domain provider.

Diane.freaney@icloud.com and my other private e-mails work well. E-mails go into my spam folder occasionally, sometimes from a mailing list, which I find it easy to unsubscribe, sometimes e-mail I want that I just have not added the e-mail address to Contacts.

I had purchased a paid account for rootedinvesting.com when at Bainbridge Graduate Institute that included Goggle Drive and other Google tool that we were required to use. Google is a bulldog that sinks its teeth into your bank account and refuses to let go. It was hard work to get Google to relinquish its hold on rootedinvesting.com, even though NameCheap now holds the domain. I thought I had finally done it, when I started getting e-mails from a hacker, using my domain name.

I had used my Gmail account for so many years that I found it impossible to shut down. I get 300 plus spam e-mails a day. I just delete and empty trash at least once a day.

Google caused the e-mail spam problem, which I will discuss in depth in the Google chapter of this book.

Why isn't the Federal Trade Commission or some federal agency holding Google accountable for cleaning up the mess they made? I would be happy to forward my spam folder to a federal agency if the agency would assure that I never got these e-mails again.

Contacts

My Contacts have 2,487 entries. Until recently I could see some in Google and some in Apple. I just looked now and that distinction is gone. I am guessing that happened in one of the most recent updates. I just hope it is permanent.

Calendar

I found the transition from a paper calendar to an electronic calendar particularly difficult. In my PC days, I could never get the Google calendar to work. When I transitioned to Apple Calendar, folks wanted to access my calendar and I accepted. I quickly lost control of my life or so it seemed.

Again, hard work to delete the ancillary calendars and get back to owning my own calendar. Still Apple insists that I have a Family Calendar. Often Apple decides what should go into the Family Calendar, which means the event I have scheduled goes into never-never land and I am forced to hunt for it.

Recently Calendar is working like a calendar should, in my humble opinion. I hope it stays that way.

Messages

I have learned to text and am happy to do business with folks that I know using text. Recently politicians and some companies have decided that it is okay to contact me by text.

Let me be very clear:

—If you are a politician and you have the audacity to contact me by text, I will vote for your opponent and block you from further texts.

—It you are a corporation, I will block you and report you to the Better Business Bureau and anyone else that will listen.

Facetime

FaceTime was a big deal for a while, but now most folks who are making an impromptu unscheduled call will prefer a phone call. Just remember to leave a message if you are not a frequent caller. I block any calls from numbers not in my contacts that don't leave a message.

Find My Phone

Brilliant! I am constantly misplacing my phone. Now I have a small over-the-shoulder phone case where I try to keep my phone at all times when I am away from home.

Books

I have tried to like Books, but it is a losing battle. For Apple geeks like me, Books is part of the software package that comes included with Apple iPhones, iPads, laptops, and desktops.

I have always had trouble learning Apple software. I think it is because my mind works like Dan Bricklin and VisiCalc. For Dan, VisiCalc was a means to an end, the end being a good grade at Harvard for class participation. Dan also grew up in the family printing business. He learned to be resourceful from a very early age. VisiCalc made it possible for his father to estimate and bid printing jobs more accurately and in less time.

I tried to purchase my first e-book, **COMPLEXITY = CORRUPTION |
Big Tech 5 | Amazon** on iBooks and I honestly cannot figure out
how to do that. Books makes me appreciate the Kindle app even
more.

iCloud

I pay $9.99 a month to subscribe to iCloud and $119.88 a year from
Dropbox. I am convinced I don't need both but have not had the
time to figure out how to get rid of Dropbox and use only iCloud.

I was an early adopter of Dropbox, beta testing early features,
upgraded to Business Dropbox which quickly became
unaffordable and was unable to separate myself from Business
Dropbox when I downsized to a single person business. The
process was painful and a big time suck so my memory is fuzzy.

I have read that Photos and iCloud play well together, but have
not had time to learn how to make that happen.

Garage Band

I learned to use Garage Band at BGI MBA School and got quite good
at it. Be warned however; all these tools are great for graphic
artists and folks who have hours to spend learning them.

Keynote

Keynote is Apple's answer to Microsoft PowerPoint. TEDx Presentations, which emphasize making eye contact with your audience, have pretty much eclipsed Keynote or PowerPoint.

iMovie

I interviewed Maggy Henry about growing up in Peru and the 2,000 different varieties of potatoes and did a pretty good job until I got to the editing part. Editing is hard work for the most dedicated professional. For most of us, videos in Photos are good enough.

8 Maggy Henry talking about 2,000 varieties of potatoes grown in Peru (Watch video here: https://vimeo.com/246730564).

I shot in iMovie on my iPhone. The video is almost 15 minutes long, and would have gone longer but the battery on my iPhone died. My BGI MBA assignment was to edit down to three minutes, but what would I cut? I did upgrade to a Vimeo Pro Account for which I pay $240 annually, a good value to preserve some of my best videos.

I wondered if Andina survived the harsh on again off again ban on indoor dining that put so many fine Portland restaurants out of business. I Googled Andina Portland and learned Mama Doris has retired so no more wonderful newsletters. The younger generation, Peter and Victor Platt, have taken over. They hired a new Peruvian chef, Alexander Diestra, and serve chicha, street food-inspired takeaway.

> "To me, the word chicha means an engagement between music and food," says Diestra in a press release. "I will always remember, before going to a show, getting some street food. Chicha is colorful, chicha is loud, chicha is the experience of street food cuisine."
>
> —Hamilton, Katherine Chew. "Peruvian Restaurant Andina Returns with a New Chef and Takeout Concept." **Monthly Portland**. May 7, 2021.

Numbers

VisiCalc, Lotus 1-2-3, and Excel suffered from changes in operating systems. There was no easy way to update spreadsheets when an operating system changed. I remember buying Excel in a box and uploading it, always a long process.

Then Microsoft began pushing Microsoft 365; in fact, demanding that folks change. I only wanted Excel and Word, and I was tired of being pushed around by Big Tech. I wanted the Excel and Word that I had already paid for—and because I knew folks from Microsoft, I got my way for a while.

Numbers debuted in 2007. I had invested a lot of time learning Excel and then relearning Excel every time it upgraded. The logic in Numbers was different from Excel and more intent on making Numbers look pretty than making sure they were accurate.

Apple and Microsoft must have sensed customer's frustration because Apple offered a Microsoft Software Package (Classic Word and Excel) for installation on one new Apple devices for $125. I paid the price but, of course, it did not work as advertised even though I followed the instructions.

I called Apple's help line and help had no idea how to help. I kept asking for a supervisor and waited until one got on the line. I learned that not all supervisors are created equal.

Finally, I got a supervisor who was authorized to call Microsoft Help and together they figured it out.

Pages

I finally learned Pages when I started writing books. I taught myself to design covers in Pages, and I find it so much easier to respond to my proofreader's questions. I spend three or more hours a day writing and need a supportive tool. Pages helped me cross the great divide between good little girl accountant and activist author.

Photos

A great camera in the iPhone ProMax 12, and Photos have improved my picture taking considerably. The first selfie I ever took is my author's photo at Carson's Tavern. I know there is so much more to learn, but I am happy I have taken the first step.

iTunes, Music, Podcasts

The only podcast I have done so far was with the Tiny House Podcast Team Mark Grimes, MJ Boyle and Perry Gruber in their studio, actually a large closet with padding, in NEDSpace, Portland, Oregon's oldest co-working space.

No script - totally off the cuff - and so much fun.

Tiny House Podcast started on iTunes and now is available on so many formats.

We're Way Off the Reservation

with Diane Freaney and the Emerson Street House

What is Emerson Street House? Well we never really found out because our interview with intrepid Diane Freaney, Wall Street banker turned community advocate, roamed so far from housing and tiny houses, even we lost our way. It was a great conversation nonetheless, ranging from praising President Donald Trump, lambasting the construction trade, solving education in the US, building communities, and most interestingly: how not to build a passive solar home. Join us for one of the wildest conversations we've had in a l-o-n-g time. Even we were surprised. It's a wild and woolly walkabout through what lights Diane's fire on this episode of Tiny House Podcast!

I am not even sure what iTunes does anymore. I found Music and Podcast apps and each one competed to play the Podcast first, sometimes with advertisements.

FACEBOOK

Facebook is Good

01 Sympathy for Mark Zuckerberg

I read **The Ugly Truth** by Sheera Frenkel and Cecilia Kang. I thought to myself, Frenkel and Kang must be biased, Mark Zuckerberg can't be as bad as they have painted him.

I listened to Kara Swisher, host of Sway, a podcast produced by the New York Times, interview Ken Burns, a storyteller/filmmaker whom I follow. Seemingly out of nowhere, Ken Burns says:

> **Ken Burns:** She's the real deal. I mean, I hope Zuckerberg is in jail by then.
>
> **Kara Swisher:** [CHUCKLES]
>
> **Ken Burns:** This is an enemy of the state, and I mean the United States of America. He doesn't give a shit about us, the United States. He knows he can transcend it. He can get away to any place. And so it's just about filthy lucre, that's it. And a lot of people—
>
> **Kara Swisher:** You're going to love my memoir, Ken.

> **Ken Burns:** I'm sure I am. Because these people —
> and Sheryl is a complicit — the Nuremberg of this, is
> if it ever happens, which it won't, will be pretty
> interesting. The way that we've been able to
> temporize and say, oh, it's okay, we'll just go a little
> bit further. Right?

Whoa!

Up until now, I personally have found Facebook and Zuckerberg only mildly annoying. Many Facebook friends joke about being in Facebook jail, almost as if it is a badge of honor. I think I have avoided Facebook jail but how can I be sure? I do remember unfriending some on Facebook after the last Presidential election. After my unfriending spree, my Facebook friends numbered around 500, down from a high of 1,000.

I just looked now and I have 1,583 Facebook friends. I am careful to add selectively new Facebook friends, my feeble attempt to deter hackers. I am 100% certain that I have not added over 1,000 new Facebook friends since the last Presidential election. Did Facebook go back and refriend the Facebook friends I had unfriended without asking me?

I do know I only hear from a small number of Facebook friends at any given time. Is that because I have been shadow-banned? Or is it because some of my Facebook friends have a life outside of

Facebook? I always wish Happy Birthday to my Facebook friends. Sometimes that will awaken a slumbering friend; most often not.

Finally, there are the popular board games that bars run to entice customers to hang out and drink beer and eat bar snacks on slow nights. I have heard that a popular category is Rhymes with Zuck. There are real words, in Webster's Dictionary or an Urban/Street Slang Dictionary, that Rhyme with Zuck, expect for vowels—a, e, i, o, u. The most popular, of course is the F-word.

02 Facebook Is My Happy Place

I was not an early adopter of Facebook or any social media platform. I became aware of Facebook during my theater and independent film period, but saw little use for Facebook in my daily life.

In 2010, I enrolled at Bainbridge Graduate Institute (BGI), a hybrid MBA program in Sustainable Systems. Classes met weekly online and monthly for an intensive weekend at Islandwood, a nature preserve on Bainbridge Island.

We learned to work online in teams, a skill which I never really mastered. I found Lynda.com, an online learning platform, and signed up for the Facebook course. I managed to muddle through and was proficient for a month or two before Facebook instituted changes. My 70-plus-year-old brain processes information differently than my fellow BGI students, who were mostly under 35.

Social media was among the most popular course at BGI, because we needed the skills we learned in the social media class in order to excel or at least muddle through all our other classes. One assignment was to build a Facebook Page. The Facebook Page still exists, or did the last time I looked, and some folks still post to it. I am an admin on this site and two other sites but I have no clue how to access them anymore.

BGI taught us how to be "influential," actually political, but I didn't realize it at the time. BGI was progressive liberal if I had to put a label on its politics. I began to see that some of the tactics BGI taught us were offensive to some of my Facebook friends so slowly I began to back off and look at how I interacted with Facebook differently.

Now Facebook is my happy place. My Facebook friends are artists, who post their art and their friend's art. Artists typically support each other, happy when another artist sells a piece or gets a commission. Their art adds beauty to my life. I avoid artists who focus on the dark side.

My niece posts photos with her son, celebrating birthdays, first and last days of school, and other events that warrant a celebration. Friends celebrate births with baby photos, and death with a story of what a friend or relative meant to them during their life. Photos of family reunions, birthday parties, graduation parties, football games, any event where folks gather together.

Pets photos are big - new puppy and kitten antics, obituaries for dogs and cats who cross over the rainbow bridge, and introducing rescue dogs to their new digs. Memories of my grand dog Daphne come up all the time, reminding me of what a comfort she was to me during my foot surgeries in Portland, Oregon.

Food is art and really good food is great art. I eat out at least one meal a day, a necessary respite for those of us who work at home during the day. I was so sad when the restaurants were closed due to COVID. I was one of the first customers when local restaurants reopened. I post my meals online and have quite a following among my foodie friends.

I have included some photos from Facebook friends and family that have created my happy place.

03 The Barn Theatre—Stuart, Florida

Community Theatre is my first love, not as a performer because, until recently, people with limited ability were not welcome on stage. I am the audience - you need me - is my favorite line.

The Barn Theatre, the local community theater in Stuart, Florida, is walking distance from my home on the medical mile, if I could walk that is, which is difficult due to Charcot-Marie-Tooth. Good parking, small theater (160 seats), great volunteer staff, and cold water for sale.

3 The Barn Theatre's Instagram page.

The Full Monty was the first show of the '21-'22 season. The show takes place in Buffalo, NY, after the steel mills closed. The men are out of work and the women are bringing home the bacon.

The men devise a scheme to make a ton of money in one night, rent an auditorium for one night to perform a Chippendale-like show, where the men strip and the women throw money at them. Except some of the men keep getting cold feet and the promoter is afraid they wouldn't show so he wanted $1,000 deposit, a lot of money in those days.

Jerry Lukowski's son, Nathan, goes to the bank, withdraws $1,000 from his college fund and gives it to his Dad for the deposit. Nathan said he expects to double his money, a great return for one night. The men promise The Full Monty (full frontal nudity). The men keep their promise, very tastefully.

Community theater and all low budget performing arts venues use Facebook, Instagram and whatever free and low cost options for advertising.

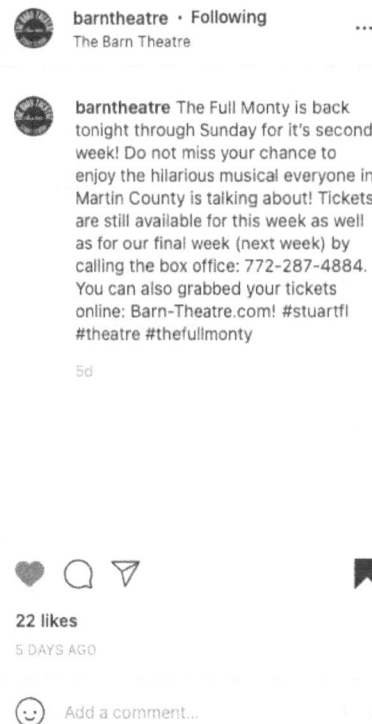

barntheatre · Following
The Barn Theatre

barntheatre The Full Monty is back tonight through Sunday for it's second week! Do not miss your chance to enjoy the hilarious musical everyone in Martin County is talking about! Tickets are still available for this week as well as for our final week (next week) by calling the box office: 772-287-4884. You can also grabbed your tickets online: Barn-Theatre.com! #stuartfl #theatre #thefullmonty

5d

22 likes
5 DAYS AGO

Add a comment...

4 Jerry and Nathan Lukowski, "The Full Monty"

04 Gillian Kennedy Wright

I met Gillian at the Institute for Cultural Advancement at the Cultural Council of Palm Beach County, an in-person professional development program that finished just before COVID struck.

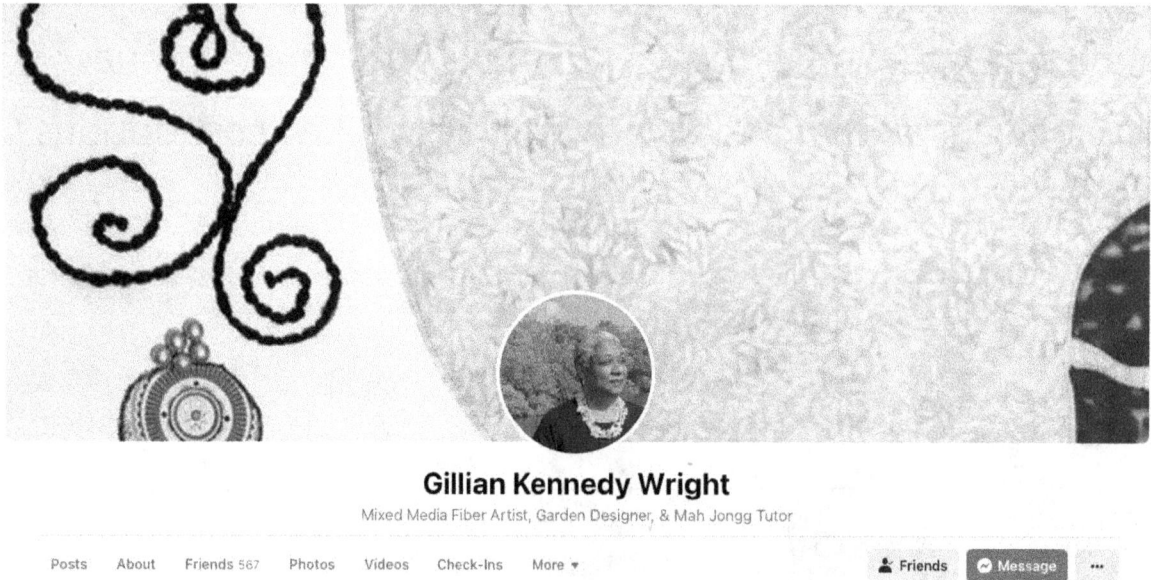

Gillian Kennedy Wright
Mixed Media Fiber Artist, Garden Designer, & Mah Jongg Tutor

Posts   About   Friends 567   Photos   Videos   Check-Ins   More ▾   👤 Friends   💬 Message   ⋯

5 Gillian Kennedy Wright's Facebook cover.

Gillian was about to embark on a journey to make her living as a full time artist. She has her studio in her backyard garden, ideal since Gillian is also an awesome gardener.

Gillian's Facebook Page says it all for me. Every morning, I look forward to opening up Facebook and being treated to pearls of wisdom from Gillian. A great way to start the day.

Kennedy Wright Designs
October 7 at 7:35 PM · 🌐

Ubuntu...the belief that we all are defined by our compassion and humility towards others.

6 Kennedy Wright Designs--ubuntu

05 John Prince Park Preservation Facebook Page

I look forward to posts from John Prince Park Preservation (JPPP) every morning. Amazing photography: sunrises, sunsets, local wildlife, water sports on Lake Osborne, folks along the trail, dogs, cats, a great cross section of life along the trail.

Lynn Anderson ▸ My Sky Photo
★ Favorites · 8h · 🌐

9-21-21 Sun came up for a few seconds this morning...now raining cats and dogs!

7 John Prince Park Preservation Instagram post.

My neighbor, Lynn Anderson, an admin on the page recruits new folks—those who will add to the rich photography and others like me who enjoy nature photography.

Omar Becerra, a hair, color and make-up stylist on Clematis Street in West Palm Beach, is also a great photographer. Omar recently moved to Lake Osborne and had added his photography art to

JPPP. The cover photo for the Facebook e-book is Omar's photo of "ducks watching karate squirrel devoured their lunch."

06 Stuart Main Street

I am a proud member of Stuart Main Street (SMS). I was able to join as a friend for $50.00, which is what I can afford since my fledging businesses have yet to make any money. Fortunately, some more established businesses can afford a higher membership level which (I hope) supports the meager budget, including a part-time executive director.

The About section of SMS's Facebook Page indicates nonprofit organization and includes the following:

> "A 501c3 nonprofit organization with a mission to create and promote a positive downtown experience for residents, businesses and visitors. Embracing the future while preserving the past. "

SMS is a business membership organization, 501 c3 is a paragraph in the Internal Revenue Code. Stop confusing people. Businesses can deduct SMS dues as a business expense. Stop with the 501 c3 mumbo jumbo already.

09 Stuart Main Street Haunted House Instagram.

And if you really want to go the membership route, consider a cooperative membership organization, as conceived by Martin Luther King, Jr.

Keep up the good work Stuart Main Street!

Stuart Main Street is in Downtown Stuart Florida.
September 29 at 8:15 AM · 🌐

Get Spooky with our friends at Stuart Heritage Museum, Inc..They are offering Ghost Tours on Oct 9.
You even get to use some paranormal equipment to find some ghosts! 👻

For more info visit, https://bit.ly/3zPFyHa.

WICKEDCITYGHOSTTOURS.COM
Stuart Feed Supply Museum History Mystery Ghost Tour | Wicked City Ghost To
This event combines local history with the paranormal in Stuart's oldest commercial buildin...

Facebook is Evil

01 Liar, Liar, Pants on Fire

"We are not actually doing what we say we do publicly."

"Facebook routinely makes exceptions for powerful actors."

"This problem is pervasive, touching almost every area of the company."

—From internal Facebook documents provided by Facebook

to the Wall Street Journalists assigned to The Facebook Files investigation. I recommend reading all the articles of The Facebook Files - see resources for a complete list.

As I read the words above from **The Facebook Files**, the children's ditty came to mind, "Liar, liar, pants on fire, a nose as long as a telephone wire." I can imagine mark Zuckerberg as Pinocchio with his nose getting longer every day.

Here we go Pinocchio, September 21, 2021 headline in **Wall Street Journal**:

> "Facebook Oversight Board Launches Review of Company's XCheck System"
>
> Inquiry prompted by **Wall Street Journal** investigation into social-media giant's treatment of high-profile users.

Quicker turn-around on great investigative journalism reporting than I have ever seen in the past. For example, the Boston Globe Spotlight Team's investigative reporting on the Catholic Church allowing abuse by priests for years was issued in 2002; in 2003 the **Boston Globe** received a Pulitzer Prize for Public Service "for its courageous, comprehensive coverage....an effort that pierced secrecy, stirred local, national and international reaction and produced changes in the Roman Catholic Church." And still the sexual abuse cases keep coming, most recently at the Vatican in Rome, reported by the **Washington Post**, July 21, 2021.

My point is that before the social media explosion, it took years for real change to happen. Not anymore. Mark Zuckerberg has created the vehicle of his demise. The Facebook community is already in revolt —wait until the word spreads about the XCheck System.

At first I thought it weird that **The Facebook Files** said nothing about former President Donald Trump and the Trump family. Then I remembered that good investigative journalists only report the facts that they garner from long periods of reviewing documents that they obtain from freedom of information act (FOIA) requests. Trump called out Facebook and all the social media types in public—no need to report on secret memos. I do note that Mark Elliott Zuckerberg's Wikipedia page includes a photo of Zuckerberg with President Donald Trump at the White House on September 19, 2019. Nice touch Zuck!

The Facebook Files investigative team has done its job. Now they can move on to another assignment secure in the knowledge that people like Ken Burns and ordinary folks like you and me will demand justice and continue to hold Zuck's feet to the fire.

02 Is Sheryl Sandberg A One-Trick Pony?

With Sherry Sandberg, COO Facebook, and Mark Zuckerberg's second in command for many years, the phrase one-trick-pony comes to mind.

Sheryl graduated from Harvard (AB) and Harvard Business School (MBA). Larry Summers, Harvard economist, became her thesis advisor and her mentor. She followed Summers to the World Bank, and to US Treasury, where she became his chief of staff, and then to the Clinton Administration. When Summers left in 2001, Sandberg moved on to Google.

Sandberg made Google profitable by growing online advertising. She joined Facebook and did the same thing. Sandberg followed the Harvard MBA playbook exactly as she was taught at Harvard.

I remember my own brief time at Harvard, when I learned about other people's money (OPM). At the time, I remember envisioning a group of well-fed sheep following a pied piper off a cliff to certain death. That is exactly what happened in the 2008 global financial crisis. As has happened so many times in the past, the perpetrators of the crisis dusted themselves off, banded together, and mostly survived and even prospered. The working stiffs of the world suffered.

Sheryl Sandberg's one trick was public relations - testifying before Congress, issuing press releases, speaking with reporters and making excuses for Facebook, which Sandberg expected the public to swallow hook, line and sinker. And when challenged she became a raging maniac.

From Sandberg's Wikipedia page:

The New York Times published a report in 2018 detailing Sandberg's role in handling Facebook's public relations after revelations of Russian interference in the 2016 United States elections and its Cambridge Analytica data scandal. Soon after, on November 29, 2018, the New York Times reported that Sandberg had personally asked Facebook's communications staff to conduct research into George Soros's finances days after Soros publicly criticized tech companies, including Facebook, at the World Economic Forum. In a statement, Facebook said the research into Soros "was already underway when Sheryl [Sandberg] sent an email asking if Mr. Soros had shorted Facebook's stock."

According to the **Wall Street Journal**, during a meeting, Mark Zuckerberg blamed Sandberg personally for the outcome of the Cambridge Analytica scandal, stating that Zuckerberg "blamed her and her teams for the public fallout over Cambridge Analytica," and that Sandberg "confided in friends that the exchange rattled her, and she wondered if she should be worried about her job."

The January 6, 2021 United States Capitol attack seemed to do Sheryl Sandberg in. I read that Sandberg resigned, but then the resignation seemed to be withdrawn. It would make sense for her to take an extended leave of absence. She did not take time off after her second husband Dave Goldberg's sudden death. Now she is about to get married and merge two families with five children. An extended leave of absence would also protect Sandberg from the media. HR would be prohibited from releasing any information under employee privacy rules. Sandberg's Wikipedia page still shows her as COO, Facebook (2008 - present).

Ironic, isn't it? Privacy rules protect Sandberg from being held accountable for Facebook violating the privacy of ordinary folks who believed them when Facebook told us they would protect our privacy.

03 Ken Burns on Sway Podcast

A.   Ken Burns regarding Mark Zuckerberg on Sway Podcast

> ". . . I mean, I hope Zuckerberg is in jail by then.

> "This [Zuckerberg] is an enemy of the state, and I mean the United States of America. He doesn't give a shit about us, the United States. He knows he can transcend it. He can get away to any place. And so it's just about filthy lucre, that's it. And a lot of people—"

Ken Burns knows his history and always gets his facts straight, so I dug around to see what I could find. In May 2021, many sources reported that Zuckerberg (and Chan) purchased an additional 600 acre for $53 million on the Hawaiian island of Kauai. Zuckerberg Chan already own 100 acres on Kauai, creating some enemies in the process. Zuck keeps purchasing more properties, allegedly for conservation and privacy, but how much privacy does one family need?

B. Ken Burns regarding Sheryl Sandberg on Sway Podcast

"I'm sure I am. Because these people — and Sheryl is a complicit — the Nuremberg of this, is if it ever happens, which it won't, will be pretty interesting. The way that we've been able to temporize and say, oh, it's okay, we'll just go a little bit further. Right?"

The **Oxford English Dictionary** defines complicit as involved with others in an illegal activity or wrongdoing, as an example, 'all of these people are complicit in some criminal conspiracy.'

The Nuremberg Code, a set of research ethics for human experimentation was one outcome of the WWII Nuremberg Trials:

1. The voluntary consent of the human subject is absolutely essential.

2. The experiment should be such as to yield fruitful results for the good of society, unprocurable by other methods or means of study, and not random and unnecessary in nature.

3. The experiment should be so designed and based on the results of animal experimentation and a knowledge of the natural history of the disease or other problem under study that the anticipated results will justify the performance of the experiment.

4. The experiment should be so conducted as to avoid all unnecessary physical and mental suffering and injury.

5. No experiment should be conducted where there is an a priori reason to believe that death or disabling injury will occur; except, perhaps, in those experiments where the experimental physicians also serve as subjects.

6. The degree of risk to be taken should never exceed that determined by the humanitarian importance of the problem to be solved by the experiment.

7. Proper preparations should be made and adequate facilities provided to protect the experimental subject against even remote possibilities of injury, disability, or death.

8. The experiment should be conducted only by scientifically qualified persons.

9. During the course of the experiment the human subject should be at liberty to bring the experiment to an end if he has reached the physical or mental state where continuation of the experiment seems to him to be impossible.

10. During the course of the experiment the scientist in charge must be prepared to terminate the experiment at

any stage, if he has probable cause to believe, in the exercise of the good faith, superior skill and careful judgment required of him that a continuation of the experiment is likely to result in injury, disability, or death to the experimental subject.

I am thinking Ken Burns may be referring to… Sandberg…complicit…Nuremberg. Perhaps Burns is referring to Zuck's push to get America vaccinated, or Instagram's toxicity to teenage girls. Ken Burns is a deep thinker. I am guessing we will learn soon.

The Facebook Files, A Wall Street Journal Investigation

Facebook Inc. knows, in acute detail, that its platforms are riddled with flaws that cause harm, often in ways only the company fully understands. That is the central finding of a Wall Street Journal series, based on a review of internal Facebook documents, including research reports, online employee discussions and drafts of presentations to senior management.

Time and again, the documents show, Facebook's researchers have identified the platform's ill effects. Time and again, despite congressional hearings, its own pledges, and numerous media exposés, the company didn't fix them. The documents offer perhaps the clearest picture thus far of how broadly Facebook's problems are known inside the company, up to the chief executive himself.

I feel like I have been hiding under a rock about Facebook. Facebook has been under fire for such a long time and I have been oblivious to the problems. I read Sheryl Sandberg's Lean In: Women, Work, and the Will to Lead when I was in at Bainbridge Graduate Institute (BGI). I thought it was interesting that a woman finally broke through the glass ceiling and that she hired a ghost writer to tell her story.

I had worked my ass off, first married and then as a single mother, and not had the same results that Sandberg seems to think all women could have if they just leaned in, which I think she means try harder.

It seems like we are in for a wild ride.

01 Facebook says its Rules Apply to All. Company Documents Reveal a Secret Elite that s Exempt

> Mark Zuckerberg has said Facebook allows its users to speak on equal footing with the elites of politics, culture and journalism, and that its standards apply to everyone. In private, the company has built a system that has exempted high-profile users from some or all of its rules. The program, known as "cross check" or "XCheck," was intended as a quality-control measure for high-profile accounts. Today, it shields millions of VIPs from the company's normal

enforcement, the documents show. Many abuse the privilege, posting material including harassment and incitement to violence that would typically lead to sanctions. Facebook says criticism of the program is fair, that it was designed for a good purpose and that the company is working to fix it.

The photo I chose for the Facebook cover design is by Omar Becerra, for John Prince Park Preservation. Omar titled his photo "helplessly they watch karate squirrel eat their food." Omar is currently in Facebook Jail, with 2 more days to go. I asked a FB friend was Omar in jail for making an anti-vac statement? My FB friends said no, anti-communist.

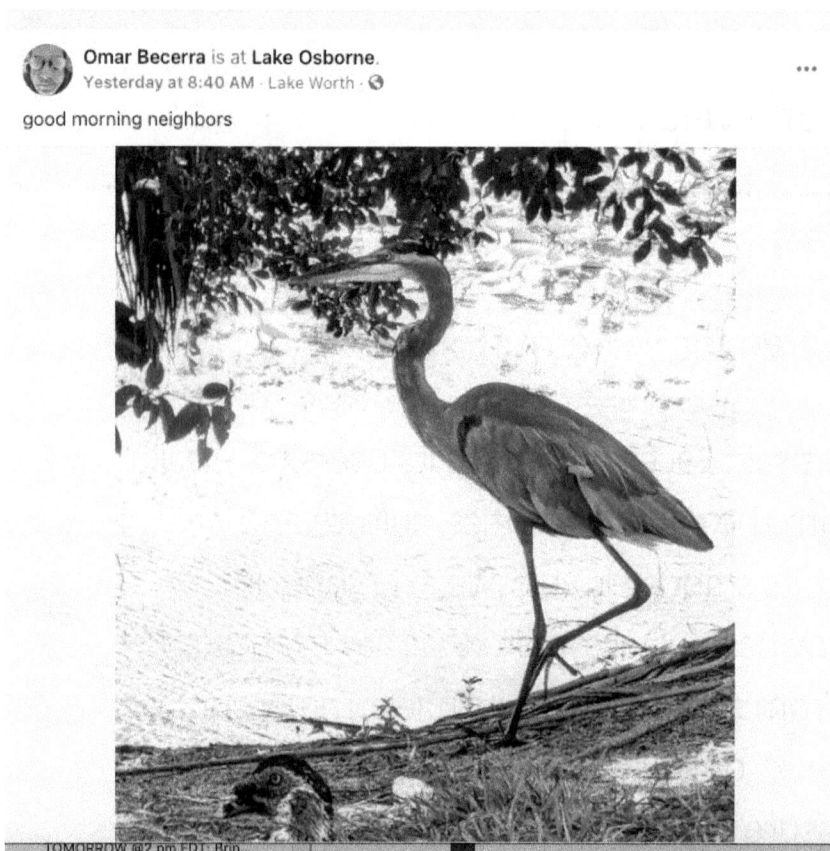

11 Omar Becerra: John Prince Park Preservation (Instagram).

But of course, Omar grew up in Cuba, under Castro. He knows what it is like to be really, really poor without proper housing and healthy food. Omar still has family in Cuba so he is sensitive to his family's needs. His brother in Cuba had COVID and recovered without medicine. His brother had to recover on his own because Cuba is a poor country and cannot afford vaccine.

Omar has been a licensed cosmetologist in Florida since 1984, and California since 2002. Currently, Omar owns and operates a hair and make-up salon on Clematis Street in West Palm Beach, where he is the solo stylist.

Omar loves children and animals as is evident in his Facebook posts. Facebook needs to stop giving a free pass to politicians, celebrities and other jackasses that are trying to control ordinary citizens and start supporting people like Omar.

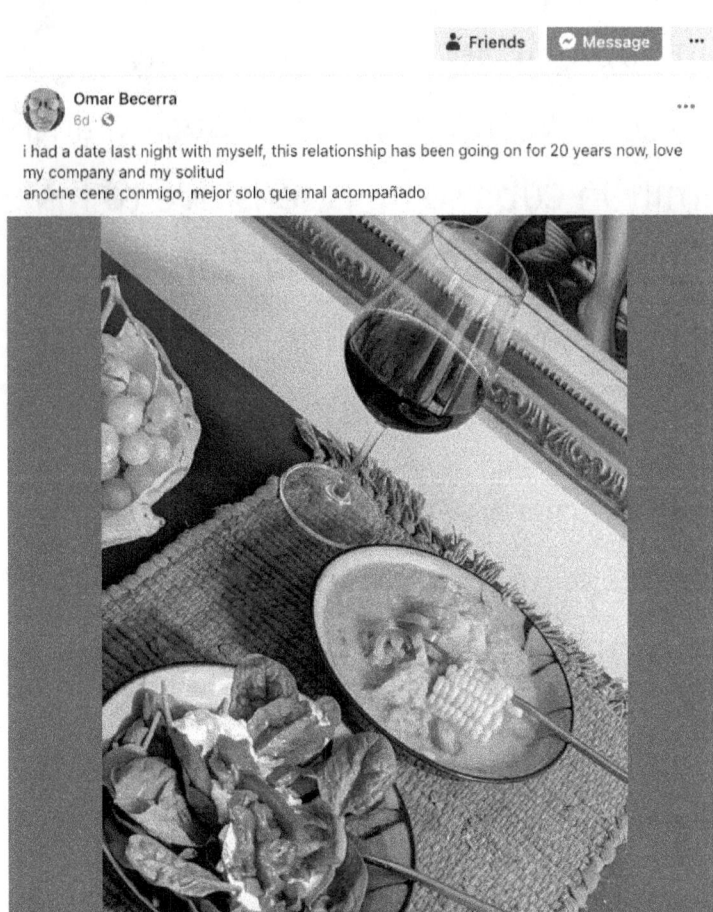

Friends   Message   ...

Omar Becerra
6d · ⊙

i had a date last night with myself, this relationship has been going on for 20 years now, love my company and my solitud
anoche cene conmigo, mejor solo que mal acompañado

12 Omar Becerra: date with himself post.

Oh, and what about the American citizens who have opted out of not just Facebook, but all technology? Like Brunhilde, the building Nazi at the over-55 condominium on Lake Osborne where Omar is my neighbor. Brunhilde doesn't own a smartphone or an Internet connection. I am not even sure she reads paper books.

Brunhilde's husband ran away with another woman, leaving her to raise their children on her own. This seems to have filled Brunhilde's heart with hate. Hate that she continues to drag around and project on other women, like my upstairs neighbor

Gwen Alexander, a wonderful neighbor who has since passed, and me.

Several folks in my Lake Osborne community, local churches, and local watering holes, have told me that Brunhilde bad mouths me with everyone she meets. Brunhilde is now Vice President of our over-55 condo board, which she seems to think makes her the supreme commander, able to rule the lives of everyone in our condo.

Brunhilde hates ducks, trees, flowers, anything that grows it seems. She keeps a broom handy to whack the ducks and break their eggs. She hates flowers and trees, and would rather have brown grass than allow a condo resident to plant and care for flowers.

But I digress… Facebook says it is working to fix the "secret elite that's exempt" problem. And this time Zuckerberg says they really, really mean it.

From where I sit, hell will freeze over first.

02 Facebook Knows Instagram is Toxic for Many Teen Girls, Company Documents Show

Researchers inside Instagram, which is owned by Facebook, have been studying for years how its photo-sharing app affects millions of young users. Repeatedly, the company found that Instagram is harmful for a sizable percentage of them, most notably teenage girls, more so than other social-media platforms. In public, Facebook has consistently played down the app's negative effects, including in comments to Congress, and hasn't made its research public or available to academics or lawmakers who have asked for it. In response, Facebook says the negative effects aren't widespread, that the mental-health research is valuable and that some of the harmful aspects aren't easy to address.

Unpacking this statement is not on my wheelhouse. I am 78 years old, with no young children in my life. I only go to Instagram occasionally. For example, the Director of The Full Monty at the Barn Theatre in Stuart, Florida, told me excellent photos of the cast were posted on Instagram.

Jonathan, a young gay, black, Mexican man, who is also an anti-vaxxer, built up a following of 4,000 plus fellow anti-vaxxers on Instagram. Anti-vaxxing is a NO-NO in Zuck's world and suddenly Jonathan found he was shadow-banned. I guess I am also an "anti-vaxxer" since I follow a different protocol than the recommended vaccines. Still Jonathan's words were foreign to me, so I went to Wikipedia:

> Shadow banning, also called stealth banning, ghost banning or comment ghosting, is the practice of blocking or partially blocking a user or their content from an online community so that it will not be readily apparent to the user that they

have been banned. For instance, shadow-banned comments posted to a blog or media website will not be visible to other users accessing the site.

Somehow this cut into Jonathan's revenue stream. Jonathan sells water filtration systems, with his mother as his only employee, so he was able to stay afloat financially. Jonathan went back to Instagram and asked to have his followers restored and Instagram refused. So he joined TikTok and tried to recreate his followers from memory, Now the Chinese government is restricting TikTok.

Jonathan suggestion I name this series Fuck Zuck, with a subtitle Zuck Sucks. I said all my e-books are good and evil of the Big Tech 5, from my personal experience. I am pleased that the **Wall Street Journal** has created **The Facebook Files**, providing factual information that the US Congress is using to grill Facebook.

03 Facebook Tried to Make its Platform a Healthier Place. It got Angrier Instead.

Facebook made a heralded change to its algorithm in 2018 designed to improve its platform—and arrest signs of declining user engagement. Mr. Zuckerberg declared his aim was to strengthen bonds between users and improve their well-being by fostering interactions between friends and family. Within the company, the documents show, staffers warned the change was having the opposite effect. It was making Facebook, and those who used it, angrier. Mr.

Zuckerberg resisted some fixes proposed by his team, the documents show, because he worried they would lead people to interact with Facebook less. Facebook, in response, says any algorithm can promote objectionable or harmful content and that the company is doing its best to mitigate the problem.

Poor Zuck, he never learned that Facebook is a tool, not a destination. As the pandemic wanes, folks are craving in-person user engagement. Facebook is a good place to announce an event, and maybe allow folks to indicate an interest, but mostly people want to be with people.

Just ask Barbra Streisand.

> People,
> People who need people,
> Are the luckiest people in the world
> We're children, needing other children
> And yet letting a grown-up pride
> Hide all the need inside
> Acting more like children than children

04 Facebook Employees Flag Drug Cartels and Human Traffickers. The Company s Response is Weak, Documents Show.

Scores of Facebook documents reviewed by the **Wall Street Journal** show employees raising alarms about how its platforms are used in developing countries, where its user base is huge and expanding. Employees flagged that human traffickers in the Middle East used the site to lure women into abusive employment situations. They warned that armed groups in Ethiopia used the site to incite violence against ethnic minorities. They sent alerts to their bosses about organ selling, pornography, and government action against political dissent, according to the documents. They also show the company's response, which in many instances is inadequate or nothing at all. A Facebook spokesman said the company has deployed global teams, local partnerships and third-party fact checkers to keep users safe.

Again, not in my wheelhouse, and, if Facebook is going to go into developing countries, it must be in Facebook's wheelhouse, or just retreat and shut down activity in those countries.

Nasty stuff.

05 How Facebook Hobbled Mark Zuckerberg s Bid to Get America Vaccinated

Facebook threw its weight behind promoting Covid-19 vaccines—'a top company priority, 'one memo said—in a demonstration of Mr. Zuckerberg's faith that his creation is a force for social good in the world. It ended up demonstrating the gulf between his aspirations and the reality of the world's largest social platform. Activists flooded the network with what Facebook calls 'barrier to vaccination 'content, the internal memos show. They used Facebook's own tools to sow doubt about the severity of the pandemic's threat and the safety of authorities main weapon to combat it. The Covid-19 problems make it uncomfortably clear: Even when he set a goal, the chief executive couldn't steer the platform as he wanted. A Facebook spokesman said in a statement that the data shows vaccine hesitancy for people in the U.S. on Facebook has declined by about 50% since January, and that the documents show the company's 'routine process for dealing with difficult challenges.'

I am grateful to live in Florida where vaccinations are optional. I think it is great that Chan Zuckerberg Initiative makes vaccines available - at least I think CZI does.

Vaccines have helped many people, vaccines have also harmed many other people. In fact, most folks I know that have been vaccinated lost at least one day of work. Folks with healthy immune systems who contracted COVID became ill, stayed home and in bed, as with the flu, and recovered quickly, with fatigue being the most long lasting symptom. If a healthy person stayed in bed for a week to ten days, with no exercise, I guarantee that person would be fatigued.

One good thing that has come out of the pandemic, if you are sick or even think you might be sick, you are encouraged to stay home. Remote working has made that possible, a permanent change to our work/live balance.

06 Facebook s Effort to Attract Preteens Goes Beyond Instagram Kids, Documents Show

Facebook has come under increasing fire in recent days for its effect on young users. Inside the company, teams of employees have for years been laying plans to attract preteens that go beyond what is publicly known, spurred by fear that it could lose a wave of users critical to its future. Why do we care about tweens? said one document from 2020'. They are a valuable but untapped audience. Adam Mosseri, head of Instagram, said Facebook is not recruiting people too young to use its apps—the current age limit is 13—but is instead trying to understand how teens and preteens use technology to appeal to the next generation.

Psychological games Facebook plays with children. Most Silicon Valley parents restrict their children's use of the Internet, so why is it okay to manipulate the offspring of the masses? To keep the offspring of the masses enslaved perhaps? To create Internet factories to replace the Industrial Revolution factories?

07 Facebook's Documents about Instagram and Teens, Published

A Senate Commerce Committee hearing about Facebook, teens and mental health was prompted by a mid-September article in the Wall Street Journal. Based on internal company

135

documents, it detailed Facebook's internal research on the negative impact of its Instagram app on teen girls and others. Six of the documents that formed the basis of the Instagram article are published here.

Suicide! Suicide!

The nasty side effect no one is talking about. Suicide at all ages—because the isolation of lockdown made some people crazy, much crazier than normal. In Florida, you have to be careful if you talk suicide because you can be Baker Acted. Even children can be Baker Acted, which means they lock you up for a couple of days of a week, then send you back into the situation you came from.

08 Is Sheryl Sandberg's Power Shrinking? Ten Years of Facebook Data Offers Clues

The **Wall Street Journal** team for **The Facebook Files** deals in facts so I get that they have to document everything.

Sheryl Sandberg is a one-trick pony. She does not have another trick up her sleeve. It is time for Sandberg to go home to her palace in Menlo Park, California, be a full time housewife and mama to the blended family of five children with her new husband and write books, using traditional publishing without a ghost writer.

The Facebook Files

01 Rule #1: Stop Being Political

Facebook spent $20 million in federal lobbying expense last year, more than any other US company. Amazon was close behind ($18 million) and the other Big Tech 5—Microsoft ($9.4 million), Google ($7.5 million), and Apple ($6.7 million).

Issie Lapowskys 'October 16, 2020 article in **Protocol** offers the facts: "Here are the top political donors from Amazon, Apple, Facebook, Google and Microsoft. Only one is backing Trump."

The article does not include the contribution of $600,000 to Elect President Biden by the Emerson Collective LLC, a company controlled by Laurene Powell Jobs. The Emerson Collective owns a majority stake in **The Atlantic**, which alleged that Trump referred to soldiers who died in World War I as "losers" and "suckers."

That really pissed Trump off and prompted a Trump tweet, "Steve Jobs would not be happy that his wife is wasting money he left her on a failing Radical Left Magazine that is run by a con man."

People who track such things say that the Big Tech 5, actually all of Silicon Valley, supported Elect President Biden/Harris with cold hard cash.

I am curious, has Biden/Harris worked out for them? From where I sit, not very well. It seems to me that the Trump administration was much more supportive of technology and business, when Trump was in office.

The way I see, if you force US citizens to take sides, roughly 50% will vote Democratic and 50% will vote Republican, as has happened in recent presidential elections. In reality, all US citizens are individuals and will never agree 100% with the dogma of either Democrats or Republicans.

How to solve the political donation dilemma? Just stop corporations, their employees and families from making political donations.

What can go wrong? Crooked politicians will corner big tech executives and let them know that they will propose and vote for laws which are detrimental to their business. Are all politicians crooked? Certainly not, but enough are that our government (federal, state, county, city, town, etc.) is in the mess we are in today.

What is the solution? I would start by requiring folks who wish to make political donations to make them through the IRS (Internal Revenue Service), via their Federal Income Tax Return Form 1040. The IRS would collect the money and distribute to political candidates or political parties, as directed by the US tax payer on Form 1040.

The IRS, in cooperation with the US Treasury, delivered stimulus checks to the intended recipients mostly on time and to the correct individual. Sure there were some mistakes, late deliveries, and some fraud, but things improved dramatically with each new stimulus check.

The IRS could eliminate candidates 'bookkeeping headaches in reporting political donations, anonymous individual donations and total donations to candidates and parties in summary. Candidates could budget accurately because the IRS would tell the candidate which day each quarter their funds would be delivered to their bank account. And, of course, non-cash donations would be prohibited.

I suggest allowing each individual to contribute $300 annually on Form 1040. Facebook and other companies who want to contribute more to support our democracy could put money into a giant PAC, controlled by the Internal Revenue Service. The IRS could be empowered to offer up to $300 each to low income folks who are unable to afford to contribute to political candidates. Offer first to registered voters and, if there are any funds left, as an incentive to low income folks who register to vote.

We will be producing an e-book on the US Election System sometime next year. Our readers often have the best ideas on how to change broken systems. Please send us your ideas.

Email Diane Freaney at thecatlady@dianefreaney.com or snail mail 850 NW Federal Highway 411, Stuart, FL 34994.

02 Rule #2 Chan Zuckerberg Sells Facebook Stock

It is time for all endowments, and CZI is an endowment, to sell all holdings in stock and bonds, including Facebook, and invest in US Treasuries. I think I read somewhere that China was the largest investor in US Treasuries. That is about to end, as the bankruptcy of China Evergrande Group is on the horizon. A friend asked me if Evergrande is China's Enron. Perhaps it is. And the demise of yet another large CPA firm Price Waterhouse Coopers for Evergrande, as Arthur Anderson was in Enron.

There are still other factors at work. Chinese citizens expect higher wages as they lust after goods and services they have provided cheaply to the rest of the world. This pushes up the cost of exports and creates a trade imbalance. China needs the funds invested in US Treasuries back in Chinese banks.

Still the liquidation of CZI stocks and bonds must be gradual; dumping it all at once would create chaos in the markets and ultimately hurt small investors and their retirement accounts. I recommend a ten-year/forty-quarter plan, liquidating uniformly over forty quarters, so that at the end of it, CZI is 100% invested in US Treasuries.

03 Rule #3 Chan Zuckerberg as a Membership Cooperative

From an op-ed piece by Doug O'Brien President and CEO, NCBA CLUSA, on January 20, 2020, Dr. Martin Luther King's birthday:

> One of the strategies that Dr. King and the Civil Rights Movement used—and that those who advocate for racial and economic justice still favor—is the cooperative business model. By coming together to own and control their own businesses, people can meaningfully participate in their economy, creating stable jobs, building community wealth, and inspiring democratic participation.

Facebook is ideally suited to become a membership cooperative, at least in the United States. Perhaps US citizenship could be a requirement to join the US membership cooperative.

The structure is SIMPLE.

- One vote for each member.

- Basic dues $2.00 a month or $12.00 annually, paid online.

- Tiered sponsorship levels - for example, CZI may want to sponsor Facebook at the $1 billion level.

- Profits, if any, are split, on some predetermined level. I recommend the Alberta Co-op accounting system as a model. Individual members pay taxes, or not, depending on their tax brackets.

Look at MeWe as an example [from Mark Weinstein's Op-Ed Piece]:

> Two years ago the platform had five million users and no revenue. Today it has nearly 20 million users and is breaking even with millions of dollars in revenue.

I tried to join MeWe after the 2020 election, at the paid level ($4.99 a month) but dropped it quickly because I did not have the time to learn this new platform. I just joined again at the free level, and will explore that first before I decide to join at the paid level. I do note that MeWe Groups can be shared on Facebook and Twitter.

04 Rule #4 Quit When You are Ahead

This one is for me! Just as I was going to send the e-book out for proofreading, an article by Jeff Horwitz, came across my screen: "The Facebook Whistleblower, Frances Haugen, Says She Wants to Fix the Company, Not Harm It."

> On May 17, shortly before 7 p.m., [Frances Haugen] logged on for the last time and typed her final message into Workplace's search bar to try to explain her motives. 'I don't hate Facebook,' she wrote. 'I love Facebook. I want to save it. '

That is how I feel. I have a love/hate relationship with all Big Tech 5, in fact most of the Silicon Valley companies.

> You've got to accentuate the positive
> Eliminate the negative
> Latch onto the affirmative
> Don't mess with Mister in Between.
>
> —Songwriters: Mercer John H / Arlen Harold

Ac-Cent-Tchu-Ate the Positive lyrics
© The Johnny Mercer Foundation, Harwin Music Co.

Addendum

11 Facebook Whistleblower Comes Clean on "60 Minutes"

Frances Haugen reveals her identity to Scott Pelley on "60 Minutes," ahead of her testimony this week before the Congressional committee investigating Facebook.

60 Minutes Whistleblower
↗ 63K people are talking about this

CBS ✓
13h · ⊕

60 Minutes interviewed Facebook whistleblower Frances Haugen, who says political parties have been quoted in Facebook's own research saying they know Facebook changed its algorithm and "now if [they] don't publish angry, hateful, polarizing... content," there's less engagement. For the full report, click here: https://cbsn.ws/3DdzHxw

Facebook's written response to 60 Minutes can be read here: https://cbsn.ws/3a3HQba

We know our constituents don't like this.

60 Overtime

👍❤️😮 607   178 Comments 754 Shares

👍 Like   💬 Comment   ↗ Share   😀▾

12 Facebook whistleblower, Frances Haugen, on CBS's "60 Minutes"

Why did Frances Haugen come forward? Her attorney, John Napier Tye, Founder and Chief Disclosure Officer, Whistleblower Aid intended to invoke The Dodd-Frank Act, which protects Haugen, as a whistleblower. Before he founded Whistleblower Aid, John N. Tye was a whistleblower himself. A graduate of Yale Law School, Tye decided to publicize his allegations against the U.S. National Security Agency (NSA) in a completely legal way.

Why is Frances Haugen's message on "**60 Minutes**" so powerful? Frances has empathy for Mark and says exactly what Facebook's problem is in her own words. I am 100% sure the **Wall Street Journal** team assigned to **The Facebook Files** was accurate in their reporting and kept the whistleblower's name secret. Yet the public has become wary of media outlets because of the fake news problem.

13 Online coverage of the Facebook whistleblower story.

Following Frances Haugen's appearance on Sunday, the first person I met at breakfast on Monday and Tuesday mornings, sat down at my table and ranted on about a problem they have experienced. Neither man is a Facebooker and both men had heard of the Facebook whistleblower. Both men told amazing stories, which I will cover in future e-books.

14 Wildflowers Live—"The Centripetal Velocity of Jessica Su

...a YouTube video by hosts Patti Lucia and Taylor Callahan, has a conversation with Jessica Su, currently at Roblox, formerly Facebook. Jessica Su's work at both Roblox and Facebook centers around children and safety online. Jessica Su gives her perspective as a Team Leader on Internet Safety. I encourage you to watch the video.

GOOGLE

The United Republic of Google

Trump Elected President (November 8, 2016)

<u>My Election Night 2016</u>

It was 7:00 p.m. or so on election night. I was in a long-awaited meeting with two women leaders of the Japanese American community about the exhibit of the art of Jimmy Tsutomu Mirikitani, which was hanging in my home, the Emerson Street House, in Portland, Oregon.

Jimmy was the unsung hero of the WWII concentration camps. Jimmy was at Tule Lake, the most punitive of the camps, and yet he managed to make art very day. I was anxious to have the support of the Japanese American community because I wanted as many folks as possible to see the exhibit during the short time it was in my home.

We finished our meeting and my guests asked politely if they could check out the preliminary election results on their phone. Of course, I said.

Yikes! Trump was expected to win!

My guests started crying and wringing their hands. I empathized. I had voted for Hilary, as the lesser of two evils. Trump had won, saving me from a very stupid mistake. My guests said they had to leave and walked out comforting each other.

Trump was President.

I wrote Trump a letter the very next day asking to join his staff, but only if I could continue living in Portland, Oregon. No way was I going to Washington, D.C., which I viewed as a cesspool. No response to that letter. Yeah, the guy had his hands full with a very big job so I forgave the snub.

I continued to write to Trump and, in January 2017, Trump began writing back. Well-documented policy letters on Tax Policy, Education Policy, and Student Financial Aid—stuff I am passionate about and have studied for many years. Trump's ideas were spot on, not revolutionary, just good common sense.

Zach Vorhies' Election Night 2016

Zach was deep into a programming project at Google's YouTube office in San Bruno, California. He went into the TV room to get some coffee and noticed a depressed vibe.

"Hey, guys! How's the election going?"

One guy spoke up. "Not good."

"What? Is Trump winning?"

Another guy responded. "Yeah. Big time. I think he's going to win it."

"No way," [Zach] said, "Clinton's got it in the bag."

—Vorhies, Zach; Heckenlively, Kent. (p. 15).

Zach spent election night 2016 with members of the Hive. Trump gave his victory speech. Hilary's chief of staff, gave her concession speech.

—Vorhies, Zach; Heckenlively, Kent. (p. 16).

All-Hands Meeting Thursday, November 17, 2016

An 'All-Hands' meeting took place at Google's corporate headquarters in Mountain View, CA on Thursday, November 17, 2016, which would set the stage for the company's future actions.

—Vorhies, Zach; Heckenlively, Kent. (p. 18).

A Young Google employee asked a question of Sergey Brin:

"Google's mission is to organize the world's information and make it useful. But during this election we've seen a lot of misinformation, disinformation, fake news coming from fake news websites, being shared by millions of low information voters on social media. And ultimately there's been many, many people who've been voting, who've been acting, based on completely made up information. So, can Google do anything to try to figure this out? To try to do something against this very organized, very intense campaign of disinformation targeted at low information people?"

—Vorhies, Zach; Heckenlively, Kent. (pp.34-35).

The rest of **Google Leaks** sounds like the Twilight Zone to me, possibly because I am not a computer engineer or data scientist. I recommend that you purchase Google Leaks on Amazon, as I did. From the Amazon product page for Google Leaks:

Story of Big Tech Censorship and Bias
and the Fight to Save Our Country

The madness of Google's attempt to mold our reality into a version dictated by their corporate values has never been portrayed better than in this chilling account by Google whistleblower, Zach Vorhies. As a senior engineer, Zach watched in horror from the inside as the 2016 election of Donald Trump drove Google into a frenzy of censorship and political manipulation. The American ideal of an honest, hard-fought battle of ideas—when the contest is over, shaking hands and working together to solve problems—was replaced by a different, darker ethic alien to this country's history as wave after of censorship destroyed free speech and entire market sectors.

Working with New York Times bestselling author Kent Heckenlively (Plague of Corruption), Vorhies and Heckenlively weave a tale of a tech industry once beloved by its central figure for its innovation and original thinking, turned into a terrifying "woke-church" of censorship and political intolerance. For Zach, an intuitive counter-thinker, brought up on the dystopian futures of George Orwell, Aldous Huxley, and Ray Bradbury, it was clear that Google was attempting nothing less than a seamless rewriting of the operating code of reality in which many would not be allowed to participate.

Using Google's own internal search engine, Zach discovered their real "AI-Censorship" system called "Machine Learning Fairness," which he claims is a merging of critical race theory and AI that was secretly released on their users of search, news and YouTube. He collected and released 950 pages of these documents to the Department of Justice and to the public in the summer of 2019 through Project Veritas with James O'Keefe, which quickly became their most popular whistleblower story, which started a trend of big whistleblowing.

From Google re-writing their news algorithms to target Trump to using human tragedy emergencies to inject permanent blacklists, Zach and Kent provide a "you are there" perspective on how Google turned to the dark side to seize power. They finish by laying out a solution to fight censorship. Read this book if you care to know how Google tries to manipulate, censor, and downrank the voice of its users.

My Most Important Takeaway

"The officer looked both relieved and amused, saying, 'Okay, I guess his story checks out,' and the remaining police started treating me like a good guy. I heard one of them mutter under his breath, 'Fucking Google,' as the tension completely drained out of the situation. The boys in blue didn't have much love for the tech lords of Silicon Valley."

—Vorhies, Zach; Heckenlively, Kent. (p. 212).

BackRub and Early Google History

Brin and Page met at Stanford and quickly became intellectual soulmates and close friends. They built BackRub, a webcrawler, in their Stanford dorm rooms, and used Stanford's computer resources.

I am guessing they figured out that Stanford would own BackRub if they continued at Stanford so they suspended their Ph.D. studies, incorporated as Google, Inc., and moved into Susan Wojcicki's garage in Menlo Park. The ubiquitous garage where all successful businesses start.

> The name "Google" originated from a misspelling of "googol", which refers to the number represented by a 1 followed by one-hundred zeros. Page and Brin write in their first paper on PageRank: "We chose our systems name, Google, because it is a common spelling of googol, or 10100 and fits well with our goal of building very large-scale search engines."
>
> —History of Google - Wikipedia.

According to Wikipedia, Susan Wojcicki was Google's first Marketing Manager in 1999. Susan handled two of Google's largest acquisitions — the $1.65 billion purchase of YouTube, an online video platform, in 2006 and the $3.1 billion purchase of DoubleClick, an Internet ad servicing company, in 2007.

Sergey Brin married Susan's sister Anne Wojcicki in 2007. They had two children and divorced in 2015.

What is PageRank?

From Wikipedia:

> PageRank (PR) is an algorithm used by Google Search to rank web pages in their search engine results. It is named after both the term "web page" and co-founder Larry Page. PageRank is a way of measuring the importance of website pages. According to Google:

> PageRank works by counting the number and quality of links to a page to determine a rough estimate of how important the website is. The underlying assumption is that more important websites are likely to receive more links from other websites.

> Currently, PageRank is not the only algorithm used by Google to order search results, but it is the first algorithm that was used by the company, and it is the best known. As of September 24, 2019, PageRank and all associated patents are expired.

Yikes! I had never heard of PageRank and as of September 24, 2019 PageRank and all associated patents are expired.

What does that mean to me, a dedicated user of Google Search? And what do those other algorithms do to Google Search? How do I know if I am getting really news or fake news? Do the Googlers even care?

Okay back to my personal stories and experience with Google—good and evil and my recommendations on how Google needs to change.

Google is Good

oo Google is Good

I am having trouble focusing on Google is Good now that The Facebook Files have surfaced so much negativity impacting humanity and threatening our democracy.

I find it helpful to look at where the Big Tech 5 started, at least from where I sit.

Amazon = online book store

Apple = hardware and software for the creative community

Facebook = online high school and college yearbook

Google = algorithms

Microsoft = business software

Algorithms are the devil incarnate, in my humble opinion. Google Search, the feature I like best about Google, is based entirely on algorithms, the features I like least in the Land of the Internet.

I will tiptoe forward with trepidation, always aware that fake news is the enemy.

01 Google Search

A colleague told me Google search is a card catalog, not an authoritative source. Got it!

In July 1999, I wrote "**A New Model for the Creative Use of College Endowments to Reduce College Tuition**," my master's project for the Organizational Dynamics program at the University of Pennsylvania.

I had to go to the library and use the physical card catalog to do research for my project. I was working full-time and commuted into Philadelphia from the suburbs so there were few occasions when I had time, and Penn's library was open. Research was tedious and boring.

Fortunately, the **Philadelphia Inquirer** ran a series in April 1996, that explored the issues around student financial aid and endowments in public and private universities. I collected copies of The Philadelphia Inquirer with the article, which informed my work. I finally completed my master's project just in time to graduate in August 1999.

As I embark on my career as an activist author, Google Search is a Godsend. Most of my e-books are short-form non-fiction, and reference Internet sources for historical and current facts. I write from my own experience and that always has to be in the context of the larger picture.

Even using Google Search requires some expertise, just as using an old fashioned library card catalog requires knowledge of the system. I have not studied SEO (search engine optimization), which I think is important for marketing. Right now I am concentrating on avoiding fake news stories in my e-books.

The **Wall Street Journal** is my go-to source for good reporting and factual information. The newspaper industry has deteriorated through mergers and become increasingly partisan.

I get so frustrated with the clunky login features. For example, I pay for the **Washington Post** and the **Palm Beach Post**. I see an article in Facebook from one of these sources that I want to read, click on it and immediately hit a paywall.

Grrr! I don't have the time or the patience to wade through their stupid login feature. I get angry and move on. Note to self - cancel subscriptions to the **Washington Post** and the **Palm Beach Post** next time I have a minute.

I have noticed that important issues that I follow appear in many different publications, sometimes directly from another media publication, other times a unique perspective from a team of journalists.

For example, the Florida Bar Association report with recommendations for changes in condominium law aimed at preventing another Surfside condo tragedy. I first saw an article from the **Miami Herald** in Facebook, click on it and hit the paywall. I decide to pay for a subscription. Surfside is in Miami Dade and - I reasoned - the **Miami Herald** would have the most interest in seeing sound new condominium laws. I signed up, entered my credit card and waited to read the article. No such luck - still a paywall.

Grrr! I do get an e-mail welcoming me to the Miami Herald, with a link if I want to cancel. I cancel. I get an e-mail saying the **Miami Herald** has never heard of me. So I go back to my old standby - the Wall Street Journal.

Google Search usually does bring up all the options, particularly if I keep asking. In fact, it is easier to use Google Search than most library searches, or perhaps I just need to learn another system.

I just downloaded and installed DuckDuckGo, an alternate search engine recommended by my neighbor Lynn Anderson.

From the DuckDuckGo web site:

"Tired of being tracked online? We can help.

We don't store your personal info. We don't follow you around with ads. We don't track you. Ever."

Check out my newsletter The Snarky Express, for more on DuckDuckGo.

02 Gmail

Google Mail (Gmail) launched April 1, 2004, according to Google. Prior to Gmail, e-mail addresses were linked to an internet carrier like BellSouth, or Yahoo or AOL. When you moved it was difficult to keep your e-mail address if it was linked to BellSouth. Easier if you had Yahoo or AOL. Both have a history of being hacked.

As an early adopter, I set up my personal Gmail account - dfreaney@gmail.com. Google started advertising business addresses.

As an example, I was building the Emerson Street House, a Passive Net Zero home in Northeast Portland, Oregon. I purchased a URL through NameCheap, www.emersonstreethouse.com. Name Cheap did not offer private e-mail at the time so I went back to Google and signed up for a free e-mail diane@emersonstreethouse.com.

Google had no criteria for opening an account, so accounts proliferated, security was pretty much non-existent. Next thing I know, my Apple laptop slows to a crawl and I cannot work.

I am still not sure what happened. I know it took several days to figure out the problem and get my computer back in working order.

Somehow the e-mail created a looping system that kept recreating itself - a vicious mess. Google could easily have solved the problem but, like all the Big Tech 5, Google chose profit first, leaving its customers to wallow in the mess Google created.

03 Google Maps

Great idea! Not so great delivery!

I remember a day trip to Mount Hood from Portland, Oregon. My friend Lisa was driving. Lisa had come to rely on Google Maps to get her to her destination. Lisa had no paper maps in her car.

Google Maps took us on a wild goose chase, on the wrong side of the river and driving in circles. We blindly followed the directions, until I noticed that we had passed the same barn at least twice before.

Finally, we found a gas station that had maps for sale. We bought a map, laid it out on the counter as we paid and the kindly gas station attendant gave us directions to Mount Hood. We felt like stupid idiots. The kindly gas station attendant assured us we were not the only ones. Several people a week stopped by with the same problem.

Google is Evil

BB Google Ad-Sense

I don't understand the Google ad system and have no interest in learning more.

I listened to an interview of Sundar Pinchai, CEO Google, by a Wall Street Journal editorial staffer, and learned that Google had recently reduced its commission on ads to 15% from 22-44%.

I was thrilled to hear Sundar say Google voluntarily reduced ad commissions. Political and legal solutions always take too long and no one wins.

CC Google s Legacy List"

Google has a feature which allows you to share data with someone you name "3 months after your Google Account becomes inactive". I think it is meant to be a legacy feature like Facebook and some other social media sites are including.

Google has a list of 45 items, which I think are apps from the Google Play Store. I just wasted six hours trying to figure out what these names on the list are. I learned that Google changes the names so often that most Googlers have no idea what is Google and what is not.

Don't bother reading the next 45 sections unless you are really masochistic. Go instead to the next section, Google Needs to Change. I will list my recommendations for change. Feel free to add your own.

Write to Sundar Pinchai, Google CEO. Sundar says he wants to improve the customer experience. Tell Sundar how he can improve your experience.

Google needs to change

AO Where is Google today?

As I see it, Page and Brin are each in a giant Google "o" in the middle of the Pacific Ocean - Brin circling clockwise; Page circling counterclockwise; both spinning out of control.

Perhaps Brin and Page are chasing Mark Zuckerberg and his newly ordained Meta Platform Inc., parent or child of the old Facebook Inc. Zuck seems like Peter Pan and the lost boys. Zuck doesn't want to grow up and thinks this change will keep him young and filled with magic dust.

The Silicon Valley techies are busy creating virtual worlds with avatars to replace the human experience or so it seems to me.

The techies are out of touch with reality as human and other living beings are going in the opposite direction. Ordinary folks are longing to be together in person, enjoying parties, festivals, concerts and other events.

National Parks and outdoor recreation facilities are packed. Unemployment is at an all-time low, with many good jobs unfilled. Folks are retiring early, packing their stuff into an RV and hitting the road or just staying put and enjoying the towns they live in. Staycations are at an all-time high.

The pandemic taught us we can live with less. The big cities with long commutes are not as attractive as the small towns, often the place where we grew up. Church suppers, Friday night football games, local bars, restaurants and coffee shops.

Jeff Bezos seems to be the only Big Tech founders who recognizes the problem. Bezos acknowledges that the average life span of a public company is 25 to 30 years. Bezos said he just hopes Amazon will still be Amazon on his death (or something like that).

Amazon is also the only Big Tech 5 company that is gracefully becoming an adult, leveling off, profits were down for the most recent quarter. It is not humanly possible to keep scaling upwards forever. Amazon started as an online bookstore. I see Amazon building out its self-publishing business and enhancing the features of its online bookstore.

I also see Amazon working with competitors in its inventory and delivery system. For example, I ordered an item from Amazon and agreed to my specific delivery day, ten days out. The item was delivered from my local Walmart the very next day by Uber delivery.

Enough!

What do I want from Google?

A1 Clean Out Gmail Spam and Crap Forever

Google controls Google cloud where Google junk mail resides. I get 3 to 5 times as much spam and crap mail a day as I do e-mail that I want. Many of my friends and colleagues tell me that is their experience also.

I want Google to set up a place where folks go upload the spam and crap e-mail we get each day. Google's algorithm can sort the collected spam and e-mail and boomerang the spam and crap e-mail back to the senders.

Certainly Google has the expertise to do this now. Why don't they? I am guessing they think these folks are their advertisers and their advertisers will be offended.

The spammers and crappers are masters in imitating real companies - big banks, big box stores, etc. That crap comes along with the sexual innuendos and inappropriate stuff that we don't want our children to deal with.

Ask me what advertisements I want to receive - for example special toothpaste or cleaning supplies or chocolate and what stores I want to receive them from - local within five miles, delivery only, etc. And require that all advertisers are labeled from a mailing list and give an option to unsubscribe.

The advertising business will change—no more stupid ads—many more targeted ads that results in purchases. Isn't that what the business is supposed to be?

A2 Google Search Needs to Respect Privacy

Privacy is a thing these days. Apple started it, then I saw Facebook come out with something, I am guessing Amazon, Google and Microsoft will be next. My apologies if I missed announcements.

I am a transparency freak so I never worry about privacy, but I respect other folks' needs for privacy. I hate that algorithms can usurp another's need for privacy and use it for nefarious reasons.

I spent my entire life hiding the fact that I have Charcot-Marie-Tooth disease, which I inherited from my mother. I am grateful that I am on the high end of the bell curve and only mildly debilitated.

However, I was shocked and dismayed to open a CNN report one day about five-year-old Juliana Snow, "who has a severe case of an incurable neurodegenerative illness called Charcot-Marie-Tooth disease." Five-year-old Juliana Snow wanted to die and go to heaven. I was crushed.

Yet it makes me stronger in my struggle to allow folks to opt-out of HIPAA. HIPAA was instituted because insurance companies found any reason to deny coverage for "pre-existing conditions" and any genetic disease was considered a pre-existing condition. The reality: most of us have some "pre-existing condition." Many are benign, as my case of Charcot-Marie-Tooth disease is. Research would have benefited greatly if I could have been out in the open about my "pre-existing condition."

Perhaps a cure would have been found and Juliana Snow could have lived the happy life of a five year old child.

A4 Google Get Out of My Life

I want Google out of my life permanently. Google already knows what Google systems I use. If Google doesn't know, it is time to become an adult and figure it out.

The media is already telling the world to expect more Big Tech whistleblowers. Google has the opportunity to get ahead of the curve and solve the problems the whistleblowers will lay out for the world to see.

Don't send me lame instructions on how I can turn off one system by downloading my information. I am done with that BS. The instructions are usually unclear, often downright wrong.

Fix it now!

Addendum

I finally discovered where this Legacy List is, after much angst in trying to figure out what it means. I am guessing some trust busting government agency started making noises about busting up Google so Google came up with this sloppy solution.

> GO TO: Google Account on the right hand side of the page under your photo (avatar). Click on photo (avatar), click on Manage Your Google Account.
>
> This brings up a Welcome screen.
>
> On the left hand side, click on Data & privacy; the Data & privacy screen comes up.
>
> Scroll down to Download or delete your data (almost the bottom on the right hand side).
>
> Click on Download your data and Google Takeout appears
>
> Google Takeout.
>
> Your account, your data.
>
> Export a copy of content in your Google Account to back it up or use it with a service outside of Google.

The forty-five sections appear in the same order on the Choose What To Share List [see Legacy List section]

I am clueless why Google didn't just link to this site instead of sending me on a wild goose chase.

01 Access Log Activity

Let me opt-out of Access Log Activity effective immediately.

Adopt DuckDuckGo's privacy policy:

> We don't store your personal information. Ever.
>
> Our privacy policy is simple: we don't collect or share any of your personal information.
>
> —DuckDuckGo

02 Android Device Configuration Service

Let me opt-out of Android Device Configuration Service effective immediately.

I do not have an Android Device and do not expect to in the near future.

03 Arts & Culture

Let me opt-out of Arts and Culture effective immediately.

I love arts and culture but I am not sure I need yet another place to access arts and culture. I already have excellent access on my iPhone and on Facebook.

I can always sign up if I change my mind.

04 Calendar

Delete Google Calendar from my Account effective immediately.

I use Apple Calendar exclusively and never even look at Google Calendar.

Google Calendar just confuses me.

05 Chrome

> Google Chrome is a cross-platform web browser developed by Google. It was first released in 2008 for Microsoft Windows, built with free software components from Apple WebKit and Mozilla Firefox. It was later ported to Linux, macOS, iOS, and Android, where it is the default browser. The browser is also the main component of Chrome OS, where it serves as the platform for web applications.
>
> Most of Chrome's source code comes from Google's free and open-source software project Chromium, but Chrome is licensed as proprietary freeware. WebKit was the original rendering engine, but Google eventually forked it to create the Blink engine; all Chrome variants except iOS now use Blink.
>
> —Google Chrome, Wikipedia

The explanations just blow my mind. As I see it, Google took free and open-sourced software from many sources, fashioned it into a new web browser, layered advertising on top and charged an arm and a leg for the advertising.

For me, delete Chrome permanently from all my devices.

06 Contacts

Let me opt-out of Google Contacts effective immediately.

I use Apple Contacts exclusively and Google Contacts just confuses me.

07 Crisis User Reports

> Google Crisis Response is a team within Google.org that "seeks to make critical information more accessible around natural disasters and humanitarian crises". The team has responded in the past to the 2010 Haiti earthquake, 2010 Pakistan floods, 2010–11 Queensland floods, February 2011 Christchurch earthquake, and the 2011 Tōhoku earthquake and tsunami among other events, using Google resources and tools such as Google Maps, Google Earth, Google Person Finder, and Google Fusion Tables.
>
> —Wikipedia, Google Response Team

Whoop-de-do! At least in the United States, the media has this covered.

Suggested change: Automatic opt-out of this feature, with the ability to OPT-IN, in case of a crisis anywhere in the world.

08 Data Shared for Research

Suggested change: Automatic opt-out of data share for research. Ability to opt-in at a future date.

09 Drive

Bainbridge Graduate Institute (BGI) required students to use Google Drive. I opened a paid account, with the expectation that I could use Google Drive in my work after graduation.

I set up a new e-mail account diane@rootedinvesting for my Google Drive account. Google is a bulldog and does not let go once it has your bank account information.

I am still trying to delete Google Drive and all its information from my Internet life.

10 Fit

Automatic opt-out of Google Fit.

Allow folks to opt-in to Google Fit.

I have an Apple Watch which I use to track my health. I am not interested in Google Fit.

11 Google Account

Google's My Account is more like an army of spiders, some venomous, some not. I live in fear of stepping in the wrong place and getting bitten.

Gmail, Google Drive, old addresses and subscriptions are buried in the bones of My Account. It is not easy to figure out what to keep and what to delete.

As much as I would like to be done with Google forever, I am afraid I must keep My Account until I have had time to figure out how to close out smoothly.

12 Google Cloud Search

> "Work accounts only. Google Cloud Search is only available for work accounts."
>
> —Google Search

13 Google Fi

> "Google Fi has you covered with phone plans designed to meet your data needs. Pay only for the data you use, or go unlimited. If your needs change, you can easily switch between plans."
>
> —Google Search

14 Google Help Communities

"The Google Help Communities are a place for Google users to ask questions or provide feedback about Google products and services, discuss products and services with other Google users and enthusiasts, provide tips for using Google products and services to the community, get help from other users and Google enthusiasts …"

—Google Search

15 Google My Business

"Google My Business is a free and easy-to-use tool for businesses and organizations to manage their online presence across Google, including Search and Maps. To help customers find your business, and to tell them your story, you can verify your business and edit your business information."

—Google Search

16 Google Pay

"Send money to a friend or start a group to split expenses for dinner, bills, rent, and more. Google Pay will help you do the math and keep track of who's paid."

—*Google Search*

17 Google Play Books

"Google Play Books, formerly Google e-books, is an e-book digital distribution service operated by Google, part of its Google Play product line. Users can purchase and download e-books and audiobooks from Google Play, which offers over five million titles, with Google claiming it to be the "largest e-books collection in the world". Books can be read on a dedicated Books section on the Google Play website, through the use of a mobile app available for Android and iOS, through the use of select e-readers that offer support for Adobe Digital Editions, through a web browser and reading via Google Home. Users may also upload up to 2,000 e-books in the PDF or EPUB file formats. Google Play Books is available in 75 countries."

—Google Search

18 Google Play Games Services

"Play Games Services. Help acquire, engage, and retain players with premium features like automatic sign-in, leaderboards, achievements and friends."

—Google Search

19 Google Play Movies & TV

"Google TV (formerly known as Google Play Movies & TV) is an online video on demand service operated by Google. The service offers movies and television shows for purchase or rental, depending on availability. The service initially launched in May 2011 as Google Movies and was later renamed Google Play Movies & TV following its integration into the Google Play digital distribution service in 2012."

—Google Search

20 Google Play Store

"Google Play, also branded as the Google Play Store and formerly Android Market, is a digital distribution service operated and developed by Google. It serves as the official app store for certified devices running on the Android operating system and its derivatives as well as Chrome OS, allowing users to browse and download applications developed with the Android software development kit (SDK) and published through Google. Google Play also serves as a digital media store, offering music, books, movies, and television programs. Content that has been purchased on Google Play Movies & TV and Google Play Books can be accessed on a web browser, and through the Android and iOS apps."

—Google Search

21 Google Shopping

"Google Shopping, formerly Google Product Search, Google Products and Froogle, is a Google service invented by Craig

Nevill-Manning which allows users to search for products on online shopping websites and compare prices between different vendors. Google announced at its Marketing Live event in May 2019 that the new Google Shopping will integrate the existing Google Express marketplace into a revamped shopping experience. In the US, Google Shopping is accessible from the web and mobile apps, available on Android and iOS. Google Shopping is also available in France, accessible from the web only. Like its predecessor, Google Shopping is free and requires a personal Google account in order to purchase from the platform. A colored price tag icon replaces the parachute icon from Google Express."

—Google Shopping

22 Google Translator Toolkit

"Google Translator Toolkit was [shut down on December 4, 2019] an online computer-assisted translation tool (CAT) - a web application designed to allow translators to edit the translations that Google Translate automatically generates using its own and/or user-uploaded files of appropriate glossaries and translation memory. With the Google Translator Toolkit, translators could organize their work and use shared translations, glossaries and translation memories. It allowed translators to upload and translate Microsoft Word documents, OpenDocument, RTF, HTML, text, and Wikipedia articles."

—Google Search

23 Google Workspace Marketplace

"Google Workspace Marketplace (formerly Google Apps Marketplace and then G Suite Marketplace) is a product of Google LLC. It is an online store for free and paid web applications that work with Google Workspace services and with third party software. Apps are based on Google APIs or on Google Apps Script."

—Google Search

24 Groups

"Google Groups is a service from Google that provides discussion groups for people sharing common interests. The Groups service also provides a gateway to Usenet newsgroups via a shared user interface.

Google Groups became operational in February 2001, following Google's acquisition of Deja's Usenet archive. Deja News had been operational since March 1995."

—Google Groups

Yikes!

Just when I thought Google was torturing me by adding stuff to the legacy list that even Google knows does not exist anymore, I found that I actually belong to six Google Groups, some fairly recent.

I am pleased to say that I was able to delete all six Google Groups and, with any luck, they will not repopulate later.

25 Hangouts

"Hangouts is going away soon. Switch to Google Chat now to continue your Hangouts conversations with new features."

—Google Search

"Google Chat (formerly known as Hangouts Chat) is a communication software developed by Google built for teams that provides direct messages and team chat rooms, along with a group messaging function that allows Google Drive content sharing. It is one of two apps that constitute the replacement for Google Hangouts, the other being Google Meet. Google planned to begin retiring Google Hangouts in October 2019."

—Google Search

26 Home App

"Google Nest, previously named Google Home, is a line of smart speakers developed by Google under the Google Nest brand. The devices enable users to speak voice commands to interact with services through Google Assistant, the company's virtual assistant. Both in-house and third-party services are integrated, allowing users to listen to music, control playback of videos or photos, or receive news updates entirely by voice. Google Nest devices also have integrated support for home automation, letting users control smart home appliances with their voice command. The first device, Google Home, was released in the United States in November 2016; subsequent product releases have occurred globally since 2017."

—-Wikipedia

27 Keep

"Google Keep is a note-taking service included as part of the free, web-based Google Docs Editors suite offered by Google. The service also includes Google Docs, Google Sheets, Google Slides, Google Drawings, Google Forms, and Google Sites. Google Keep is available as a web application as well as mobile app for Android and iOS. The app offers a variety of tools for taking notes, including text, lists, images, and audio. Text from images can be extracted using optical character recognition, and voice recordings can be transcribed. The interface allows for a single-column view or a multi-column view. Notes can be color-coded, and labels can be applied for organization. Later updates have added functionality to pin notes, and to collaborate on notes with other Keep users in real-time."

—Wikipedia

28 Location History

Google Latitude was a location-aware feature of Google Maps, developed by Google as a successor to its earlier SMS-based service Dodgeball. Latitude allowed a mobile phone user to allow certain people to view their current location. Via their own Google Account, the user's cell phone location was mapped on Google Maps. The user could control the accuracy and details of what each of the other users can see — an exact location could be allowed, or it could be limited to identifying the city only. For privacy, it could also be turned off by the user, or a location could be manually entered. Users had to explicitly opt into Latitude, and were only able to see the location of those friends who had decided to share their location with them.

On July 10, 2013, Google announced plans to shut down Latitude, and it was discontinued on August 9, 2013. After the feature moved to Google+ in between, Google incorporated Latitude's location sharing feature into Google Maps in March 2017.

—Wikipedia

29 Mail

I would love to delete my personal Gmail account dfreaney@gmail.com. I have diligently been alerting folks to use one of my private my e-mail accounts with some success. However, I have found that some websites have decided to use my Gmail account as my login and refuse to allow me to change to one of my private e-mails.

I get 300 to 500 unwanted e-mail every day, telling me how to enlarge my penis, ads for sex and other disgusting stuff, along with e-mails offering $50.00 to $500.00 to open an account at the Bank of Nigeria. You get the gist.

I was down for a week in 2017 after my computer was attacked by a hacker. Fortunately I found a computer consultant who was able to clean up my hard drive and get me up and running again for a $500 fee.

The buzz in Silicon Valley these days is improve the customer experience. Goggle could take a major step forward by cleaning up the offensive junk mail so many Gmail users get every day.

30 Maps

"Google Maps [launched February 8, 2005] is a web mapping platform and consumer application offered by Google. It offers satellite imagery, aerial photography, street maps, 360° interactive panoramic views of streets (Street View), real-time traffic conditions, and route planning for traveling by foot, car, air (in beta) and public transportation. As of 2020, Google Maps was being used by over 1 billion people every month around the world."

—Wikipedia

31 Maps (your places)

"Google Maps (your places) [launched February 8, 2005] is a web mapping platform and consumer application offered by Google. It offers satellite imagery, aerial photography, street maps, 360° interactive panoramic views of streets (Street View), real-time traffic conditions, and route planning for traveling by foot, car, air (in beta) and public transportation. As of 2020, Google Maps was being used by over 1 billion people every month around the world."

—Wikipedia

32 My Activity

From Google Account Overview:

All of Google, working for you

Sign in to your Google Account, and get the most out of all the Google services you use. Your account helps you do more by personalizing your Google experience and offering easy access to your most important information from anywhere.

33 My Maps

"Google Maps [launched February 8, 2005] is a web mapping platform and consumer application offered by Google. It offers satellite imagery, aerial photography, street maps, 360° interactive panoramic views of streets (Street View), real-time traffic conditions, and route planning for traveling by foot, car, air (in beta) and public transportation. As of 2020, Google Maps was being used by over 1 billion people every month around the world."

—Wikipedia

34 News

"Google News is a news aggregator service developed by Google. It presents a continuous flow of links to articles organized from thousands of publishers and magazines. Google News is available as an app on Android, iOS, and the Web.

Google released a beta version in September 2002 and the official app in January 2006. The initial idea was developed by Krishna Bharat.

The service has been described as the world's largest news aggregator. In 2020, Google announced they would be spending $1 billion to work with publishers to create Showcases."

—Wikipedia

The pesky aggregators again. The aggregators essentially pirate the work of hard working journalists and mush them together so it is hard for the reader to determine if the Google News is real or fake.

Google, hear me loud and clear. I opt-out of Goggle News. Why is it even on my list?

35 Pinpoint

"Introducing Pinpoint, a research tool from Journalist Studio.

Pinpoint is a research tool that helps you explore and analyze large collections of documents. It's simple to use, saving you time and effort so you can focus on your story."

—Google Pinpoint, Getting Started with Pinpoint

36 Profile

Your profile info in Google services

Personal info and options to manage it. You can make some of this info, like your contact details, visible to others so they can reach you easily. You can also see a summary of your profiles."

—Google Search

37 Purchases & Reservations

I found this post from three years ago on Reddit:

How do I delete Google's records of purchases and reservations I've made at non-Google sites?

While doing a security/privacy checkup today, I discovered

that Google keeps a list of purchases, reservations, etc. at myaccount.google.com.

Note that I'm not talking about purchases I made from a Google entity, or reservations I made via a Google app. They comb through your Gmail, lift the details of purchases, reservations, and subscriptions that show up in the emails, and compile a list of them for...reasons?

I don't want to get into a discussion of whether I should have known that Google would take each order confirmation email I received from Amazon.com purchases and logged it in their own separate archive. I just want to know how to delete it.

The help articles basically say that you "might" be able to delete each entry by clicking on each entry and clicking the little "i" information icon, but I have yet to find a single entry that can be deleted that way.

I have spent a couple of hours trying to figure out how to contact Google directly about this, but I've had no luck. The "contact" page seems to contain no way to actually contact them.

Also, once I've deleted these, how do I opt out from having them recorded in the future?

Thank you.

Edit: If you want to see your own history, go here: https://myaccount.google.com/preferences#subscriptions

Three years ago is ancient history in the Land of the Internet so I was unsure about what I would find. I clicked on Payments and Subscriptions and found four entries—one each from Home Depot, Target, Walmart, Powell's. Nothing from Amazon, where I make most of my purchases. I am guessing Amazon has got Google's number and figured it out.

There is a category under payment and subscriptions entitled Reservations. I clicked on that and some Delta Airlines flights and a $10.00 off coupon from Amazon come up. Curious!

38 Question Hub

From Wikipedia:

> Google Question Hub (GQH) is a knowledge market platform developed and offered by Google. As part of reducing non-existent digital media backlog, it uses various but not-known search algorithms to collect unanswered web search queries for content creators, including journalists. GQH is accessible via a registered Google search console account with a verified web property as contradict to Google Questions and Answers. However, searchers do not need to be registered with search console except a google account.

> As of September 2021, it is a beta product and is limited to the United States, India, Indonesia, and Nigeria. Google search users ask a question in specified languages such as English, Hindi and Indonesian language, and after collecting the

unanswered questions, Google lists them in GQH where publishers can then use them as the basis for new publishing articles.

39 Reminders

Even Google seems confused about Reminders. [See below] I was unable to find any with my account.

Search results for reminders

How to turn off notifications on calendars
Community forum - Google Account
4/4/2019 - I need to know HOW to turn this off immediately. I don't need Google reminding me of what is on my calendar. I have calendar **reminders** for that purpose.
112 Upvotes   11 Replies

Setting reminders in Chrome
Community forum - Google Account
8/3/2021 - I used to be able to set Google **reminders** just by typing the **reminder** in my search/URL bar in Chrome. But now when I do that it just brings up search ...
17 Upvotes

Privacy and security
Community forum - Google Account
10/12/2020 - (Friendly **reminder**: account security and password protection is your responsibility; and it is not the job of Google to do this for you.
1 Recommended answer   276 Upvotes   9 Replies

My Reminders are no longer showing up on my ...
Community forum - Google Account
7/1/2021 - My Google Calendar **Reminders** don't work anymore. They used to work fine but now they dont. I have restarted my phone, uninstalled and reinstalled the all, ...
2 Upvotes

40 Saved

I think I finally found where Google's Legacy List came from. The list is under Google Account: Data & privacy: Download and delete your data (way down in the right hand corner). Click on Download your date and the headline becomes Google Takeout.

I found three entries in saved, only one which I wanted. I saved the one that I wanted and deleted the rest.

41 Search Contributions

From Google Takeout:

Search Contributions

Your ratings, reviews, comments and other contributions to Google Search

Why do I care? Delete, delete, delete!

42 Street View

From Google Account:

Street View

Images and videos you have uploaded to Google Street View

I have not uploaded any images or videos to Google Street View

43 Tasks

I do not use this feature. Delete the file.

44 Voice

From Google Account:

Voice

Your saved Google Voice call history, messages and voicemails as well as current linked numbers.

None saved - delete, delete, delete.

45 YouTube and YouTube Music

I use Vimeo and SoundCloud to save videos and music that are important to me.

The video and music on this list can be deleted.

MICROSOFT

Bill Was Born Wealthy

The old adage - "born with a silver spoon in his mouth" - fits Bill Gates like a glove. Father Bill Gates Sr. was a high paid lawyer and Mother Mary, trained as a schoolteacher, was a super volunteer who parlayed her volunteer non-profit board positions into paid board positions.

Bill was a petulant child who preferred staying in his room reading and eating pencils to dining at the family dinner table. Older sister Kristi and younger sister Libby were the good children, following in their parent's footsteps in their personal and professional lives.

Kristi and Libby stayed connected to Mother Mary and Father Bill's alma mater, the University of Washington, and the Lakeside School, the alma mater of brother Bill, as well as Bill and Melinda Gates' children.

All the Gates children were taught community and advocacy, and to value giving back. Melinda Gates learned similar values growing up in Dallas, Texas, as the daughter of an aerospace engineer and a homemaker, raised and educated in the Catholic religion.

Mother Mary used her business connections to help Bill build Microsoft. She acted as his business strategist and his surrogate wife, making sure Bill had food in the kitchen and clean laundry.

Some say Mother Mary recruited Melinda to be Bill's wife, when Mother Mary knew she was dying of breast cancer.

Bill Gates Obsesses

Mother Mary did not cure Bill of obsessing or perhaps she felt it was one of his better qualities, as long as he was listening to her and followed her teachings.

Computer Obsession

Bill Gates started obsessing about computers when he was in middle school at Lakeside School. Bill was in public school until sixth grade, when his parents decided he should go to Lakeside, a private school in the neighborhood.

Bill was the class clown in public school, a role he relished, and wasn't sure he would have the same opportunity at Lakeside. He thought about failing the entrance exam, but his competitive nature got the best of him and he not only aced it but got one of the highest scores ever.

Budget Obsession

Bill Gates obsesses over budgets. As a twenty-five year old running Microsoft, he felt responsible for making sure that all the employees he hired could get their paychecks for one year if Microsoft failed. In the early days, Bill was often seen doing budgets on the back of an envelope as he contemplated just how much money he would need to keep his promises to employees.

Bridge Obsession

Bill's Mother Mary tried to arrange for Bill to meet the Oracle of Omaha, Warren Buffet because Buffet was arguably the greatest investor ever. Bill resisted, Bill was too busy coding. Mother Mary invited Warren Buffet to dinner when he was in Seattle, and Bill agreed to come.

When Gates and Buffet finally met, they became bridge partners and great friends. Bill likens bridge to a real partnership. You and your partner must "mind meld," a term borrowed from Star Trek...

> "A technique for the psychic fusion of two or more minds, permitting unrestricted communication or deep understanding."

Buffet's resignation from the board of the Bill and Melinda Gates Foundation in June 2021 must have been as difficult on Bill as his divorce from Melinda.

I wonder if Bill Gates and Warren Buffet are still bridge partners or if that relationship is sunsetting also.

Investment Obsession

Cascade Investment, LLC, is a private equity conglomerate founded by Bill Gates in 1995. Gates lured Michael Larsen to Seattle from Chicago to be Cascade's first and only CIO (Chief Investment Officer). Larsen is also CIO for the Bill and Melinda Gates Foundation.

I read that in May 2021, well ahead of the pending divorce, Bill Gates transferred $3 billion in stock to his soon to be ex-wife Melinda French Gates, including Deere & Co, AutoNation Inc., a Coca-Cola bottler, and a Canadian National railroad.

It seemed odd to me that Melinda would have an interest in these companies. Why the rush? Final distribution of marital assets was scheduled to take place six months after the divorce was final.

Deere and AutoNation are public companies and Cascade's holding had reached a level that the SEC (Securities and Exchange Commission) required additional reporting, jeopardizing Larsen's strategy of keeping his Bill Gates investment holdings private by flying under the radar.

Speed Obsession

Bill Gates is obsessed with speed. When he was living in Albuquerque with Paul Allen and a group of guys writing code, he would blow off steam by hitting the dessert roads of Albuquerque in his car at night and driving very fast, way over the speed limit on dark, unlit roads.

On December 13, 1977, in Albuquerque Bill was arrested on charges of speeding in his Porsche and driving without a license. Some say that Father Bill made this and other speeding violations go away.

Perhaps that is the real reason Bill has limos with drivers, even though he says it gives him more time to read and study the books and budgets in his ever present canvas bag.

Sports Obsession

Bill takes risks in sports, as he does in other areas of his life. Skiing, riding bikes, you name it. Taking risks that could easily claim his life, as mountain climbing did his teenage friend Kent Evans.

Bill plays tennis, up to nine hours straight in 106-degree heat. I wonder how many tennis partners can keep up with him.

Winning Obsession

Bill's obsession with winning comes from summer vacations at Camp Cheerio. Several prominent Seattle families rented out a resort for two weeks every summer. Father Bill was the mayor of Camp Cheerio, organizing tennis tournaments for the adults and camp games for the children.

Bill learned early that he needed to be on the winner's platform; second or third was okay but first was better. He always wanted to be first.

Toilet Obsession

Bill Gates is obsessed with toilets. In January 1, 1997, Nicholas Kristof, i journalist, wrote an article about the lack of sanitation in developing countries caused children to die from diarrhea. The article caught the attention of Bill and Melinda Gates.

In the Netflix docu-series, Inside Bill's Brain: Decoding Bill Gates, Melinda says she and Bill have a small daughter and if their daughter had diarrhea she would go to the pharmacy or the doctors and get medicine to stop the diarrhea. Bill says that in the world he lives in he knows no one who has ever buried a child who has died of diarrhea.

Bill goes on to have competitions with cash prizes for folks who can build toilets that would solve the sanitation problem without the traditional sanitation piping systems in use in the United States and other countries in the developed world.

The solutions were brilliant, but the cost was $50,000 and more, when a realistic number was $500.

Polio Obsession

Bill Gates is obsessed with eradicating polio. Polio, also called infantile paralysis since it affected mainly children, was eradicated in this country in the mid-fifties after Dr. Jonas Salk developed a killer-virus vaccine.

Bill discovered that polio was still active in some countries and set out to eradicate polio forever. Bill forged ahead without understanding local cultural values which ultimately derailed his polio project.

Vaccine Obsession

From The Real Anthony Fauci by Robert F. Kennedy Jr. (Children's Defense Fund).

> "In early 2000, Fauci shook hands with Bill Gates in the library of Gates' $147 million Seattle mansion, cementing a partnership that would aim to control an increasingly profitable $60 billion global vaccine enterprise with unlimited growth potential. Through funding leverage and carefully cultivated personal relationships with heads of state and leading media and social media institutions, the Pharma-Fauci-Gates alliance exercises dominion over global health policy.
>
> The Real Anthony Fauci details how Fauci, Gates, and their cohorts use their control of media outlets, scientific journals, key government and quasi-governmental agencies, global intelligence agencies, and influential scientists and physicians to flood the public with fearful propaganda about COVID-19 virulence and pathogenesis, and to muzzle debate and ruthlessly censor dissent."

During the pandemic, Gates, Fauci and Big Pharma pushed expensive and unproven vaccines, while denigrating readily available and inexpensive therapies like Ivermectin which had been used successfully for many years.

Money Can Not Buy More Time

Bill Gates can buy anything he wants except more time. Bill is acutely aware of this so he makes sure he makes every minute count.

Lauren Jiloty, has been Director Executive Administration of Gates Ventures since November 2011, according to her LinkedIn profile. Prior to that she was Assistant to Hilary Rodham Clinton in the US Department of State and US Senate (March 2005), and Assistant to Bob Graham, US Senate (November 2002).

Lauren appears to be Bill's scheduler. She knows exactly where he is at all times. Lauren says Bill is always on time, never even a minute late.

He always carries a large canvas bag filled with budgets and books he is currently reading or wants to read. Lauren is responsible for seeing the bag is cleaned often and contains the books he wants. She says he is particularly concerned that his books are organized when he is traveling because he reads so much on trips.

Bill also schedules two Think Weeks a year, a reading vacation, usually at a cabin in the woods on Hood Canal.

Bill Gates' Brain is Complex

The second episode of **Inside Bill's Brain: Decoding Bill Gates**, starts off with filmmaker David Guggenheim telling Melinda French Gates the series is called Inside Bill's Brain and Melinda starts laughing hysterically.

Melinda says the inside of Bill's brain is chaos; there is always so much going on at once. That is why he goes on think weeks so he can quiet his mind, synthesize his thoughts, and lead in the way he wants to lead.

Melinda says Bill's brain is chaos with so much complexity all the time. Bill likes complexity; he thrives on complexity.

A basic premise of all my work is...

Complexity = Corruption

The solution is to always simplify.

Therein lies the difficulty with Microsoft.

Pivotal Ventures – a Melinda French Gates Company

Quotes from the Pivotal Ventures website, followed by my analysis of meaning:

> "Founded by Melinda French Gates in 2015, Pivotal Ventures advances social progress in the United States through investment, partnership, and advocacy."

Melinda's children were at Lakeside School, Bill's alma mater, the school of the Bezos children and science teacher Dan Jewett, MacKenzie Scott's, formerly Bezos, now husband.

Melinda has said that she and Bill often disagree in private and always present a united front in public; so important to Melinda, public relations and marketing in the Bill/Melinda partnership.

> "We take on old problems in new ways, using philanthropic dollars and investment capital to fund transformational ideas, people, and organizations working to advance social progress. Our work is specifically focused on expanding women's power and influence and strengthening the well-being of people in the United States."

Let me translate: philanthrocapitalism operates as a for-profit, while masquerading as a charity, accepting tax deductible contributions from wealthy cronies and conducting business in a way which benefits the donors more than it benefits the alleged beneficiaries of the largesse of the donors.

"Want to learn more? Follow us on LinkedIn."

Of course LinkedIn! Melinda, the marketer again. Microsoft acquired LinkedIn in 2016, "to grow the professional networking site and integrate it with Microsoft's enterprise software, such as Office 365."

"To make progress go further and faster, we go beyond traditional philanthropy. We believe transformational ideas can come from anywhere, so we fund experimentation in promising, untested approaches. We also deploy a diverse set of funding tools, pulling on a range of levers to take on entrenched barriers."

Sounds a lot like what the Bill and Melinda Gates Foundation is doing, except this is clearly Melinda French Gates only. I wonder just how long Melinda's discontent with Bill has been festering? Bill Gates first met Jeffrey Epstein on January 31, 2011. Hmmm.

"All of our strategies are informed by partners on the frontlines of these issues, and we seek out guidance from people with lived experience of the challenges we're working to solve."

One criticism of the Bill and Melinda Gates Foundation and other philanthrocapitalistic organizations, is that they are threatening our democracy, creating a parallel government system, undermining the work of the government system created by the US Constitution.

In some ways Pivotal Ventures seems to be doing work in the same way as the Bill and Melinda Gates Foundation, except that it is focused on girls and women in the United States. Still tethered to wealthy individuals who pull the strings - sort of like puppets in a traveling show.

"Here are some of the areas we focus on:

·Women in Technology and Innovation

·Women in Public Office

·Women and Girls of Color

·Paid Family and Medical Leave

·Caregiving

·Adolescent Mental Health"

oo Microsoft is Good

Microsoft is good at selling second-rate software for too much money. Bill Gates is convinced he is the best, which he often is, and folks should just get in line and do what Bill says.

Bill Gates lacks social skills. Mother Mary made up for his weaknesses when she was around, making him stop coding and come out of his room for meals, dressing him up for interviews and speaking engagements, finding him a place to live and a housekeeper to make sure he had healthy food and the house was clean and the laundry done.

Bill's sisters thought Bill was too geeky to ever marry, but Mother Mary courted Melinda French, the perfect partner for Bill in terms of intellect and drive. Melinda and Bill married shortly before Mother Mary died of breast cancer on June 10, 1994.

Melinda kept the same crazy schedule as Bill until she became pregnant with Jenn, their first child. Then she stayed home at Bill's still under construction bachelor pad overlooking Lake Washington in Medina, Washington.

Melinda carved out family quarters because she did not feel safe alone at night with baby Jenn since Bill was traveling extensively.

But I digress . . . how is Microsoft good?

Microsoft created software that ran on personal computers (PCs), co-opting mainframe computers invented by IBM. Mainframe computers took up city blocks while PCs sat on or under desks.

Mother Mary introduced Bill to IBM CEO, a fellow board member on United Way, and she may have wanted IBM to buy fledging Microsoft. Arrogant young Bill was having none of it, he was busy coding.

01 Microsoft Bing

Microsoft Bing is a second-rate search engine, consistent with Microsoft's reputation of selling second-rate software. Bing is a METOO product and, in my humble opinion, METOOs are never as good as the original.

Also, in typical Microsoft style, Bing was foisted on Microsoft Office users without their permission. Microsoft's algorithms are not as robust and they had less data available to search.

02 Microsoft Office

The one thing I know about technology is that it moves very fast, faster than most humans, including me, can comprehend and integrate into our daily routines.

The Silicon Valley techies live, work and play with fellow techies and have no idea how the rest of the world lives, works and plays.

I only care about the United States and, most recently, the southeast coast of the United States because the culture, topography and other unique features of the rest of the United States and the world are just too much for my little brain to understand.

Even Bill Gates, who appears to have the biggest brain in the world, admits that he can only focus on a limited amount of issues at once. Bill has decided that the Bill and Melinda Gates Foundation will focus on health in the developing world.

As I see it, Bill Gates unilaterally decided to use assets developed and paid for by US citizens and devote pretty much 100% to countries outside the US, without consulting US governmental agencies charged with providing assistance to countries in the developing world.

In the meantime, I had become addicted to Excel and Word for my small business needs. I had been lured away from Word Perfect and Lotus 1-2-3 with promises of great new features and free trials.

I purchased Microsoft Excel and Microsoft Word in a box while a student at Bainbridge Graduate Institute and was happy with the software that I purchased. However, every new iteration of hardware required dramatic changes to the software, which made my purchase obsolete.

The online version Microsoft Office 365 came on the scene like a giant angry gorilla, trained to make nice. Free trials, but only if you gave up a credit card number, and no way to cancel once Microsoft had you in their clutches.

I knew some current Microsoft techies from my MBA days at Bainbridge Graduate Institute and complained. They were able to allow me to continue to use the Excel and Word in a box by some mumbo jumbo only they understood. It worked for a while but then went wonky. My friends at Microsoft had moved on so I was stuck.

I started teaching myself Apple Numbers, a slow process. Finally I hired TekMedics, local technology consultants. Joe came to my home office and did his magic to make Excel work.

When I purchased new Apple equipment, Apple advertised Word and Excel for one desktop for $125.00. I purchased it, with the mistaken understanding that it would come loaded on my new Apple Mini with M1 chip. Silly me!

I was responsible for loading Word and Excel on my Apple Mini, relying on instructions that were wrong. I called Apple support and after a couple of hours on the phone, I finally got a supervisor on the phone who helped me.

Microsoft could easily have solved the problem but - like all the Big Tech 5, Microsoft chose profits first, leaving its customers to wallow in the mess Microsoft created.

03 Microsoft Maps

Great idea! Not so great delivery!

One thing I do think the anti-trust police have missed the boat on: Technology works best in collaboration, not competition. The Big Tech companies seem to think they must provide all services themselves, eschewing collaboration with competitors.

That may be changing. Recently, General Electric (GE), Toshiba, and Johnson & Johnson announced that they would break up into two or three parts. The reported reason is that the parts are worth more that the whole.

From the New York Times, "The Week in Business: Conglomerates Break Up"...

> On Tuesday, General Electric said it will spin off its health care division in early 2023 and its energy business a year later. Only its aviation division will remain. The 129-year-old company's breakup marks an end to an era of global conglomerates.

> Other large companies, like Siemens and Honeywell International, have also pared down their businesses over the last few years, and Toshiba and Johnson & Johnson

announced last week that they would split up their businesses.

But as industrial conglomerates are breaking up, a new breed of conglomerate has emerged: Big Tech companies like Amazon and Alphabet[Google] have embraced the strategy of multiple business lines, putting odd bedfellows like books and grocery delivery, or maps and phones, under the same umbrella."

The anti-trust police are after the Big Tech 5, a new strategy may be hatching in the wings.

AA Media Conflicts of Interest?

My unofficial fact checker forwarded an article by Alan Macleod, MintPress News. The article starts out..

> "Up until his recent messy divorce, Bill Gates enjoyed something of a free pass in corporate media. Generally presented as a kindly nerd who wants to save the world, the Microsoft co-founder was even unironically christened 'Saint Bill' by The Guardian.
>
> While other billionaires' media empires are relatively well known, the extent to which Gates's cash underwrites the modern media landscape is not. After sorting through over 30,000 individual grants, MintPress can reveal that the Bill & Melinda Gates Foundation (BMGF) has made over $300 million worth of donations to fund media projects.

Recipients of this cash include many of America's most important news outlets, including CNN, NBC, NPR, PBS and The Atlantic."

Awards given directly to media outlets from the Bill and Melinda Gates Foundation include:

1. National Public Radio - $24,663,066
2. The Guardian - $12,951,391
3. and the list goes on - to total 30,000 individual grants and $300 million worth of donations.

The **Wall Street Journal** seems to be the only major publication I follow not touched by this list. Please write to me at thecatlady@dianefreaney.com if you find some I missed. I will add the media outlet to my list of trusted sources.

BB The Jeffrey Epstein Affair

Bill Gates first met with Jeffrey Epstein on January 31, 2011. The case started through Florida courts in 2005 and ended when Epstein agreed to register as a sex offender in Florida in 2010.

The **Daily Beast** articles come up when I Google "when did Melinda Gates meet Jeffrey Epstein?" The **Daily Beast** is not in my usual sources so I am going out on a limb and making some wild-ass guesses…

From an article on May 7, 2021:

> "Melinda Gates met with convicted sex offender Jeffrey Epstein alongside her husband, Bill, in New York City and soon after said she was furious at the relationship between the two men, according to people familiar with the situation."

My interpretation:: A mother with small children can smell a man who has sex with children a block away.

> "The previously unreported meeting occurred at Epstein's Upper East Side mansion in September 2013, on the same day the couple accepted the Lasker-Bloomberg Public Service Award at The Pierre Hotel and were photographed alongside then-Mayor Mike Bloomberg."

My interpretation:- The Bill and Melinda Gates marriage began unraveling that same day.

> "The meeting would prove a turning point for Gates' relationship with Epstein, the people familiar with the matter say, as Melinda told friends after the encounter how uncomfortable she was in the company of the wealthy sex offender and how she wanted nothing to do with him."

My interpretation: Melinda was able to ignore Bill's dalliances as long as they were with adults; children were a very different story.

"Gates' friendship with Epstein—who for years was accused of molesting scores of underage girls—still haunts Melinda, according to friends of the couple who spoke to The Daily Beast this week in light of the pair's divorce announcement, which had been weeks in the making."

My interpretation: The idea for Pivotal Ventures, a Melinda French Gates Company founded in 2015 was born that day.

A prediction:- Bill Gates has alienated his one true partner, wife, mother and marketing maven. His lack of social skills become more evident every day, putting him a very slippery slope.

Ao Bill Gates Should Retire from Doing

Microsoft is the giant monopoly today that David Boies fought hard to defang in the **United States v Microsoft** in 1998-2001. Per Wikipedia:

> Bill Gates said Boies was out to destroy Microsoft".
>
> In 2001, the Washington Monthly called Boies "a brilliant trial lawyer", "a latter-day Clarence Darrow", and "a mad genius" for his work on the Microsoft case.

In the end, Bill Gates did an end run around the anti-trust police, birthing a vicious, venomous octopus like creature, bigger and more corrupt that the world has ever seen.

I confess that I am listening to **The Real Anthony Fauci: Bill Gates, Big Pharma, and the Global War on Democracy and Public Health**, by Robert F. Kennedy Jr.

Robert F. Kennedy, Jr. lists his occupation in Wikipedia as anti-vaccine activist; conspiracy theorist; author; environmental lawyer. Kennedy leaves little doubt about his perspective. Yet he makes so much sense - I must sit up and listen.

Bill Gates is sixty-five. He needs to retire from doing and retreat to his now-bachelor pad on Lake Washington, play more sports, read and write books, and cohort with academic theoreticians who pontificate a lot but do nothing.

Mother Mary and wife Melinda have moved on. There is no one to prod Bill to go out in the community and do good. Bill can retreat to his childhood dream of staying in his room all day and eating pencils, with hamburgers delivered occasionally.

Women become more productive as they age; men seem to go in the opposite direction.

A1 Dr. Anthony Fauci Should Retire Immediately

In The Real Anthony Fauci, Robert F. Kennedy makes a strong case for the damage Dr. Fauci has done to public health in the United States and the world, during the HIV/Aids epidemic and more recently COVID-19.

Bill Gates and Anthony Fauci met in 2000 and began a lucrative partnership which included Big Pharma and made Gates, Fauci and Big Pharma very rich, corrupting the public health mandate which Fauci was sworn to protect.

Synopsis from The Real Anthony Fauci:

>Pharma-funded mainstream media has convinced millions of Americans that Dr. Anthony Fauci is a hero. He is anything but.

>As director of the National Institute of Allergy and Infectious Diseases (NIAID), Dr. Anthony Fauci dispenses $6.1 billion in annual taxpayer-provided funding for scientific research, allowing him to dictate the subject, content, and outcome of scientific health research across the globe. Fauci uses the financial clout at his disposal to wield extraordinary influence over hospitals, universities, journals, and thousands of influential doctors and scientists - whose careers and institutions he has the power to ruin, advance, or reward.

>During more than a year of painstaking and meticulous research, Robert F. Kennedy Jr. unearthed a shocking story that obliterates media spin on Dr. Fauci...and that will alarm every American - Democrat or Republican - who cares about democracy, our Constitution, and the future of our children's health.

>The Real Anthony Fauci reveals how "America's Doctor" launched his career during the early AIDS crisis by partnering with pharmaceutical companies to sabotage safe

and effective off-patent therapeutic treatments for AIDS. Fauci orchestrated fraudulent studies and then pressured US Food and Drug Administration (FDA) regulators into approving a deadly chemotherapy treatment he had good reason to know was worthless against AIDS. Fauci repeatedly violated federal laws to allow his Pharma partners to use impoverished and dark-skinned children as lab rats in deadly experiments with toxic AIDS and cancer chemotherapies.

In early 2000, Fauci shook hands with Bill Gates in the library of Gates' $147 million Seattle mansion, cementing a partnership that would aim to control an increasingly profitable $60 billion global vaccine enterprise with unlimited growth potential. Through funding leverage and carefully cultivated personal relationships with heads of state and leading media and social media institutions, the Pharma-Fauci-Gates alliance exercises dominion over global health policy.

The Real Anthony Fauci details how Fauci, Gates, and their cohorts use their control of media outlets, scientific journals, key government and quasi-governmental agencies, global intelligence agencies, and influential scientists and physicians to flood the public with fearful propaganda about COVID-19 virulence and pathogenesis, and to muzzle debate and ruthlessly censor dissent.

In the olden days, retirement age was sixty-five. Fauci is well passed that. Maybe the stupid mistakes Bill Gates and Fauci have made are due to the aging process, which seems to start earlier in men than in women.

A3 Conglomerates are Corrupt

General Electric, Toshiba, and Johnson & Johnson started splitting into two or more sections. Their boards figured out that the parts are worth more in the markets than the whole.

The complexity drives up administration, accounting and legal fees, and leaves so many doors open for fraud and corruption. That's why I retired my CPA (Certified Public Accountant) license. Whenever a company gets into a fraudulent situation, all the executives point fingers at the CPA, and the lawyers slink away like snakes on the grass, leaving the CPAs holding the bag.

Microsoft still revolves around Microsoft Office, a mediocre suite of business software. Spinoff the other stuff and make your investors proud.

Resources

Wikipedia is my GOTO place for factual information or at least it was until I read this article from Wikipedia co-founder Larry Sanger - Wikipedia Is Badly Biased, May 14, 2020, In Wiki, Knowledge, Internet, By Larry Sanger. For better or worse, these are the Wikipedia pages I relied on for my research.

The **Wall Street Journal** (WSJ) is, in my opinion, the least political of all major US newspapers. The Opinion Editors publish rules and stick to their rules.

The **WSJ** Tech Team - Joanna Stern, Nicole Nguyen, Christopher Mims and Julie Jargon - and Lisa Bannon, Grapevine - are my favorites.

I also read online other papers daily or occasionally - **NY Times, Washington Post, Philadelphia Inquirer, CNN, FOX, Palm Beach Post, Sun-Sentinel**, and their journalists inform my work.

Resources - Amazon

Wikipedia - Amazon

Jeff Bezos née Jeffrey Preston Jorgensen
https://en.wikipedia.org/wiki/Jeff_Bezos

MacKenzie Scott, née Tuttle, formerly Bezos
https://en.wikipedia.org/wiki/MacKenzie_Scott

Lauren Sánchez https://en.wikipedia.org/wiki/Lauren_Sánchez

Preston Bezos, first born son of Jeff and MacKenzie Bezos
https://wikiborn.com/preston-
bezos?#Preston_Bezos_Age_Birthday_Religion_And_Phone_Number

Andy Jassy https://en.wikipedia.org/wiki/Andy_Jassy

Toni Morrison née Chloe Ardelia Wofford
https://en.wikipedia.org/wiki/Toni_Morrison

Marie Antionette - "Let Them Eat Cake"
https://en.wikipedia.org/wiki/Marie_Antoinette and
https://en.wikipedia.org/wiki/Let_them_eat_cake

E-book https://en.wikipedia.org/wiki/Ebook

Paperback Books https://en.wikipedia.org/wiki/Paperback

Blue Origin https://www.blueorigin.com and
https://en.wikipedia.org/w/index.php?title=Special:Search&search=blue
+origins&ns0=1

Amazon River https://en.wikipedia.org/wiki/Amazon_River

Amazon Rainforest https://en.wikipedia.org/wiki/Amazon_rainforest

Oprah's Book Club 1.0 https://en.wikipedia.org/wiki/Oprah's_Book_Club

Library Catalog https://en.wikipedia.org/wiki/Library_catalog

The Giving Pledge https://en.wikipedia.org/wiki/The_Giving_Pledge; https://givingpledge.org

Bystander Revolution https://en.wikipedia.org/wiki/Bystander_Revolution

ITT Inc. https://en.wikipedia.org/wiki/ITT_Inc.

Newspaper Articles – Amazon

"Amazon commits $300 million for affordable housing," Philanthropy News Digest, June 18, 2021

"Bezos Day One Fund awards $106 million to help address homelessness," Philanthropy News Digest, December 10, 2020.

"Bezos's $10 billion tops 2020 list of biggest gifts," Philanthropy News Digest, January 5,2021.

"Jeff Bezos to employees: 'One day, Amazon will fail 'but our job is to delay it as long as possible," CNBC, November 15, 2018

Anderson, Nick. "MacKenzie Scott donates hundreds of millions to another surprising list of colleges," Washington Post, June 16, 2021

Coleman, Julie. "MacKenzie Scott's new husband, Dan Jewett, was a Harriton High School chemistry teacher," The Philadelphia Inquirer, , Mar 10, 2021

Fleischer, Victor. "Stop Universities From Hoarding Money," New York Times, August 19, 2015

Fowler, Geoffrey A. "The Technology 202: Amy Klobuchar gets personal on smart speakers," June 16, 2021

Fowler, Geoffrey A. "Want to borrow that e-book from the library? Sorry, Amazon won't let you." Washington Post, March 10, 2021

Goodkind, Nicole. "Activist shareholders plan to advocate for disclosure of all political spending at spring shareholder meetings," Fortune, May 12, 2021

Goodkind, Nicole. "Congress targets tech giants Apple, Google, Amazon, and Facebook in new series of antitrust laws," Fortune, June 11, 2021

Greene, Jay. "Step back like a billionaire: Previous tech titan exits offer examples for Bezos," Washington Post, July 5, 2021

Mattioli, Dana. "Amazon Demands One More Thing From Some Vendors: a Piece of Their Company," Wall Street Journal, June 29, 2021

Mattioli, Dana. "Philanthropist MacKenzie Scott, Ex-Wife of Jeff Bezos, Marries Seattle School Teacher," Wall Street Journal, March 7, 2021

McCormick, John. "Amazon Maintains Lead in Cloud Infrastructure Market," Wall Street Journal, June 28, 2021

Mims, Christopher. "Amazon Got Us Hooked on One-Day Delivery—Now Small Businesses Are Paying for It," Wall Street Journal, June 12, 2021

Nguyen, Nicole. "Fake Reviews and Inflated Ratings Are Still a Problem for Amazon," Wall Street Journal, June 13, 2021

Nguyen, Nicole. "How to Shop Online and Not Get Ripped Off," Wall Street Journal, June 20, 2021

Randazzo, Sara. "Amazon Faced 75,000 Arbitration Demands. Now It Says: Fine, Sue Us," Wall Street Journal, June 1, 2021

Safdar, Khadeeja and Mattioli, Dana. "Nike to Stop Selling Directly to Amazon," Wall Street Journal, Nov. 13, 2019

Tilley, Aaron, Mattioli, D., and Grind, K. "Amazon Primed Andy Jassy to Be CEO. Can He Keep What Jeff Bezos Built?," Wall Street Journal, , July 2, 2021

Books – Amazon

Hyde, Stephen S.S. How Jeff Bezos Can Fix Health Care: Leading the Transparency Revolution. Kindle Edition, 2020

Larsson, Steig The Millennium Trilogy: The Girl with the Dragon Tattoo, The Girl who Played With Fire, and The Girl Who Kicked the Hornet's Nest. MacLehose Press, 2020.

Mackey, John, and Sisodia, Raj. Conscious Capitalism: Liberating the Heroic Spirit of Business. Harvard Business Review Press, 2012.

Rossman, John. The Amazon Way: Amazon's 14 Leadership Principles. Kindle Edition, 2021.

Rossman, John. Think Like Amazon: 50 1/2 Ideas to Become a Digital Leader, McGraw-Hill Education, 2019.

Senge, Peter M, The Fifth Discipline: The Art and Practice of the Learning Organization. Random House LLC, 2006.

Resources – Apple

Wikipedia – Apple

Steven Paul Jobs, née Abdul Lateef Jandali, (deceased October 5, 2011) | Co-Founder of Apple, Primary Investor Pixar, Founder, NeXt. https://en.wikipedia.org/wiki/Steve_Jobs

Laurene Powell Jobs | American billionaire, businesswoman, executive and the founder of Emerson Collective | Steve Job's Widow https://en.wikipedia.org/wiki/Laurene_Powell_Jobs

Chrisann Brennan | Painter and Author |Steve Job's Partner (1972-1977). https://en.wikipedia.org/wiki/Chrisann_Brennan

Lisa Brennan-Jobs | Journalist and Author | Only child of Chrisann Brennan and Steve Jobs. https://en.wikipedia.org/wiki/Lisa_Brennan-Jobs

Paul Reinhold Jobs | Coast Guard Veteran, Machinist | Steve Jobs 'adoptive father

Clara Hagopian Jobs | Accountant | Steve Jobs 'adoptive mother

Patricia Ann Jobs | Steve Jobs 'adoptive sister

Joanne Schieble Simpson, née Joanne Carole Schieble, formerly Joanne Jandali |Steve Jobs 'birth mother

Abdulfattah John Jandali, | Steve Jobs 'birth father

Mona Simpson, née Mona Jandali, | Novelist, English professor, Steve Job's biological sister https://en.wikipedia.org/wiki/Mona_Simpson;

The Hero's Journey (book) |https://en.wikipedia.org/wiki/The_Hero's_Journey_(book)

Leave It To Beaver https://en.wikipedia.org/wiki/Leave_It_to_Beaver

Punched Cards https://en.wikipedia.org/wiki/Punched_card

Apple II https://en.wikipedia.org/wiki/Apple_II

Dan Bricklin | Co-Creator of VisiCalc, often referred to as father of the Spreadsheet https://en.wikipedia.org/wiki/Dan_Bricklin

Bob Frankston | Co-Creator of VisiCalc. Frankston later worked at Lotus Development Corporation and Microsoft https://en.wikipedia.org/wiki/Bob_Frankston

Novell, Inc. https://en.wikipedia.org/wiki/Novell

Pete Musser. https://en.wikipedia.org/wiki/Pete_Musser

Ray Noorda. https://en.wikipedia.org/wiki/Ray_Noorda

Numbers | Apple Inc. Spreadsheet, released 2007 https://en.wikipedia.org/wiki/Numbers_(spreadsheet)

Lotus 1-2-3. https://en.wikipedia.org/wiki/Lotus_1-2-3

Excel https://en.wikipedia.org/wiki/Microsoft_Excel

YouTube Videos

What is the Hero's Journey?: Pat Soloman at TEDxRockCreekPark (May 11, 2013)

Finding Joe by Pat Takaya Solomon (March 19, 2020)

VisiCalc: The First Electronic Spreadsheet A look at the original electronic spreadsheet "VisiCalc" for the Apple II. (June 12, 2012)

A Problem That Changed The World | Dan Bricklin | TEDxBeaconStreet (December 6, 2016)

Made In America Store Tour Bus Preview (August 29, 2016)

Lotus History: The First Five Years (December 6, 2009)

IBM and Lotus 1 2 3 spreadsheets (August 21, 2009)

Miscellaneous Web Pages

AcqNotes | Program Management Tools for Aerospace: The Berry Amendment

Newspaper Articles - Apple

Butler, Ed. "Should we trust big tech with our health data?" BBC News. July 15, 2021.

Demick, Barbara, "At the Made in America Store, it's a challenge to keep the aisles full." Los Angeles Times. March 8, 2017.

Gelles, David. "Laurene Powell Jobs Is Putting Her Own Dent in the Universe." New York Times. February 27, 2020.

Higgins, Tim. "Apple to Allow Media Apps to Link to Own Websites for Payment Options." Wall Street Journal. September 1, 2021.

Higgins. Tim. "Apple Cedes Ground as Larger Fights Over App Store Brew in Court, Congress." Wall Street Journal. September 2, 2021.

Holland, Kimberly. "Is My Blood Oxygen Level Normal?" Healthline.

Shedden, David. "Today in Media History: Lotus 1-2-3 was the killer app of 1983." Poynter. January 26, 2015.

Stern, Joanna, "Apple's Child-Protection Features and the Question of Who Controls Our Smartphones" Wall Street Journal. August 13, 2021.

Stern, Joanna, "iPhone 12 Pro Max Review: Bulkiest iPhone Bumps Up Camera and Battery," Wall Street Journal. November 9, 2020.

Stern, Joanna, "Apple's M1 MacBook Air and MacBook Pro Review: The Laptop's Biggest Leap in Years." Wall Street Journal. November 17, 2020.

Stern, Joanna. "How the 'Right to Repair 'Might Save Your Gadgets—and Save You Money." Wall Street Journal. August 30, 2021.

Stern, Joanna. "Wallets Are Over. Your Phone Is Your Everything Now." Wall Street Journal. September 5, 2021

Winkler, Rolfe. "Apple Plans Blood-Pressure Measure, Wrist Thermometer in Apple Watch." Wall Street Journal. September 1, 2021.

Winkler, Rolfe. "Apple Struggles in Push to Make Healthcare Its Greatest Legacy." Wall Street Journal. June 16, 2021.

Books – Apple

Brennan, Chrisann. The Bite in the Apple: A Memoir of My Life with Steve Jobs. St. Martin's Press, New York.

Brennan-Jobs, Lisa. Small Fry: A Memoir. Grove Press. New York.

Isaacson, Walter. Steve Jobs: The Exclusive Biography. Simon & Schuster, New York

Simpson, Mona. A Regular Guy. Random LLC.

Resources – Facebook

Wikipedia – Facebook

Mark Eliot Zuckerberg https://en.wikipedia.org/wiki/Mark_Zuckerberg

Priscilla Chan https://en.wikipedia.org/wiki/Priscilla_Chan

Sheryl Sandberg https://en.wikipedia.org/wiki/Sheryl_Sandberg

Catholic Archdiocese of Boston sex abuse scandal
https://en.wikipedia.org/wiki/Catholic_Archdiocese_of_Boston_sex_abu
se_scandal

Spotlight (film) (2015) https://en.wikipedia.org/wiki/Spotlight_(film)

Ken Burns https://en.wikipedia.org/wiki/Ken_Burns

Shadow Banning https://en.wikipedia.org/wiki/Shadow_banning

MeWe https://en.wikipedia.org/wiki/MeWe

Newspapers Articles – Facebook

The Facebook Files, **A Wall Street Journal Investigation**.

- Horwitz, Jeff. "Facebook Says Its Rules Apply to All. Company Documents Reveal a Secret Elite That's Exempt." Wall Street Journal. September 13, 2021.

- Horwitz, Jeff. "The Facebook Whistleblower, Frances Haugen, Says She Wants to Fix the Company, Not Harm It." Wall Street Journal. October 3, 2021.

- Wells, Georgia, Horwitz, Jeff and Seetharaman, Deepa. "Facebook Knows Instagram Is Toxic for Teen Girls, Company Documents Show." Wall Street Journal. September 14, 2021.

- Hagey, Keach and Horwitz, Jeff. "Facebook Tried to Make Its Platform a Healthier Place. It Got Angrier Instead." Wall Street Journal. September 15, 2021.

- Scheck, Justin, Purnell, Newley and Horwitz, Jeff. "Facebook Employees Flag Drug Cartels and Human Traffickers. The Company's Response Is Weak, Documents Show." Wall Street Journal. September 16, 2021.

- Schechner, Sam, Horwitz, Jeff and Glazer, Emily. "How Facebook Hobbled Mark Zuckerberg's Bid to Get America Vaccinated." Wall Street Journal. September 17, 2021.

- Wells, Georgia and Horwitz, Jeff. "Facebook's Effort to Attract Preteens Goes Beyond Instagram Kids, Documents Show." Wall Street Journal. September 28, 2021

- Wall Street Journal Staff, "Facebook Documents About Instagram and Teens." Wall Street Journal. September 29, 2021.

- Stamm, Stephanie, West, John and Seetharaman, Deepa. "Is Sheryl Sandberg's Power Shrinking? Ten Years of Facebook Data Offers Clues." Wall Street Journal. October1, 2021.

Aydin, Rebecca. "Take a tour of Mark Zuckerberg's gigantic $100 million property in Hawaii." Business Insider. July 3, 2019.

Bobrowsky, Meghan and Tracy, Ryan. "Facebook Overseers To Review Double Set Of Rules." Wall Street Journal. September 22, 2021.

Briones, Isis, "Mark Zuckerberg Buys 600 Acres in Hawaii for $53 Million." Architectural Digest. May 5, 2021

Butler, Ed. "Should we trust big tech with our health data?" BBC News. July 15, 2021

Eaglesham, Jean. "China Evergrande Auditor Gave Clean Bill of Health Despite Debt." Wall Street Journal. September 21, 2021.

Fowler, Geoffrey A. "There's no escape from Facebook, even if you don't use it." Washington Post, August 29, 2021.

Frenkel, Sheera, Confessore, Nicholas, Kang, Cecilia, Rosenberg, Matthew and Nicas, Jack. "Delay, Deny and Deflect: How Facebook's Leaders Fought Through Crisis." New York Times. November 14 2018.

Grossman, Matt. "Facebook to Halt Instagram Kids Project Amid Pressure From Lawmakers, Parents Groups." Wall Street Journal. September 27, 2021.

Harlan, Chico and Pitrelli, Stefano. "A teen was accused of abuse inside Vatican City. Powerful church figures helped him become a priest." Washington Post. July 21, 2021.

Lapowsky, Issie. "Here are the top political donors from Amazon, Apple, Facebook, Google and Microsoft. Only one is backing Trump." Protocol. October 16, 2020.

Manfredi, Lucas. "FTC signals crackdown on loopholes protecting Big Tech's unreported acquisitions." FoxBusiness. September 17, 2021.

Mitchell, Heidi. "How Hackers Use Our Brains Against Us." Wall Street Journal. September 7, 2021.

O'Brien, Doug. "On Martin Luther King, Jr. Day, lifting up co-ops as a strategy for greater equity in our economy and society." Op-Ed, NCBA CLUSA, January 20, 2020.

Perrett, Connor. "Steve Jobs would not be happy that his wife is wasting money:' Trump attacks Laurene Powell Jobs over The Atlantic report." Business Insider. October 6, 2020.

Rezendes, Michael and the Globe Spotlight Team. "Church allowed abuse by priest for years." Boston Globe. January 8, 2002.

Tracy, Ryan, Day, Chad and De Barros, Anthony. "Facebook and Amazon Boosted Lobbying Spending in 2020." Wall Street Journal. January 24, 2001.

Tracy, Ryan and McKinnon, John D. "Senators Accuse Facebook of Disregarding Research Showing Harm to Teens." Wall Street Journal. September 30, 2021.

Seetharaman, Deepa. "With Facebook at 'War, 'Zuckerberg Adopts More Aggressive Style." Wall Street Journal. November 18, 2018.

Weinstein, Mark. "I Changed My Mind—Facebook Is a Monopoly." Wall Street Journal Opinion. October 1, 2021. [Mark Weinstein is the founder of MeWe, a Facebook Competitor].

Websites and Facebook Pages - Facebook

Mark Zuckerberg | Bringing the world closer together
https://www.facebook.com/zuck

Chan Zuckerberg Initiative | A Future For Everyone
https://chanzuckerberg.com

The Made in America Stores | Gift Shop
https://www.facebook.com/madeinamericastore

The Barn Theatre
https://www.facebook.com/thebarntheatrestuart/about/?ref=page_internal

MeWe https://mewe.com

Alberta Co-Op https://alberta.coop;
  https://www.facebook.com/albertacooperativegrocery/

Podcasts - Facebook

Sway (The New York Times) - "Is Ken Burns Taking Up Too Much Space? He Doesn't Think So." Kara Swisher, Host. August 2, 2021. https://podcasts.apple.com/us/podcast/is-ken-burns-taking-up-too-much-space-he-doesnt-think-so/id1528594034?i=1000530731305

A Way With Words. "Liar, Liar, Pants on Fire Origin." Grant Barrett, Host. October 14, 2017. https://www.waywordradio.org/liar-liar-pants-on-fire/

Wildflowers Live "The Centripetal Velocity of Jessica Su." Patti Lucia and Taylor Callahan, Hosts. March 22, 2021. https://www.youtube.com/watch?v=Es8FrBXgPnw&t=476s

Books - Facebook

Frenkel, Sheera and Kang, Cecilia. An Ugly Truth: Inside Facebook's Battle for Domination,

Harper, New York. July 13, 2021.

Sandberg, Sheryl. Lean In: Women, Work, and the Will to Lead. Knopf, New York. March 12, 2013.

Zuboff, Shoshana. "The Age of Surveillance Capitalism: The Fight for a Human Future at the New Frontier of Power." Public Affairs. Jan 15, 2019.

Films

The Social Network. Screen play by Aaron Sorkin. Sony Picture Releasing. 2010. https://en.wikipedia.org/wiki/The_Social_Network

Television – Facebook

"Whistleblower: Facebook is Misleading Public on Progress Against Hate Speech, Violence, Misinformation," Segment by Scott Pelley, correspondent (Maria Gavrilovic Alex Ortiz, producers). "60 Minutes" CBS. 4 October 2021. https://www.cbsnews.com/news/facebook-whistleblower-frances-haugen-misinformation-public-60-minutes-2021-10-03/

Resources – Google

Wikipedia - Google

Google https://en.wikipedia.org/wiki/Google

Sergey Brin https://en.wikipedia.org/wiki/Sergey_Brin

Larry Page https://en.wikipedia.org/wiki/Larry_Page

Alphabet Inc. https://en.wikipedia.org/wiki/Alphabet_Inc.

Sundar Pichai https://en.wikipedia.org/wiki/Sundar_Pichai

Stanford University https://en.wikipedia.org/wiki/Stanford_University

Anne Wojcicki https://en.wikipedia.org/wiki/Anne_Wojcicki

23andMe https://en.wikipedia.org/wiki/23andMe

Esther Wojcicki https://en.wikipedia.org/wiki/Esther_Wojcicki

Stanley Wojcicki https://en.wikipedia.org/wiki/Stanley_Wojcicki

Susan Wojcicki https://en.wikipedia.org/wiki/Susan_Wojcicki

Web crawler https://en.wikipedia.org/wiki/Web_crawler

BackRub https://en.wikipedia.org/wiki/History_of_Google#BackRub

Menlo Park https://en.wikipedia.org/wiki/Menlo_Park,_California

YouTube https://en.wikipedia.org/wiki/YouTube

DoubleClick https://en.wikipedia.org/wiki/DoubleClick

PageRank https://en.wikipedia.org/wiki/PageRank

Google Chrome https://en.wikipedia.org/wiki/Google_Chrome

Apple WebKit https://en.wikipedia.org/wiki/WebKit

Mozilla Firefox https://en.wikipedia.org/wiki/Firefox

Google Crisis Response
   https://en.wikipedia.org/wiki/Google_Crisis_Response

Google Play Books https://en.wikipedia.org/wiki/Google_Play_Books

Google Play Movies & TV https://en.wikipedia.org/wiki/Google_TV

Google Classroom https://en.wikipedia.org/wiki/Google_Classroom

Newspapers Articles - Google

Cohen, Elizabeth, Heaven over hospital: Parents honor dying child's request. CNN. November 3, 2015.

Hagey, Keach and Mickle, Tripp. Google Charges More Than Twice Its Rivals in Ad Deals, Unredacted Suit Says. Wall Street Journal. October 22, 2021.

Stern, Joanna. Pixel 6 and 6 Pro: Google Says It's Serious About Smartphones. For Real This Time. Wall Street Journal. October 19, 2021.

Podcasts – Google

Google's CEO on the Future of Work. Wall Street Journal. October 18, 2018.

Google's Sundar Pichai: Excerpts From a Conversation at the WSJ's Tech Live Conference. Wall Street Journal. October 21, 2021

Books – Google

Favor, James. Google Pixel 6 And 6 Pro User Guide For All Categories: A Comprehensive Manual With Illustrations For All Categories. The Best Ever. Kindle Edition. October 22, 2021.

Vorhies, Zach and Kent Heckenlively, Kent. "Google Leaks: A Whistleblower's Exposé of Big Tech Censorship". Kindle Edition. Skyhorse. August 2021.

Uddin, Junaed Mohammed. The Complete Google Guidebook. Kindle Edition. October 17, 2021.

Websites – Google

Hive.org - Hive is the global community for purpose-driven leaders, creatives, entrepreneurs, and innovators with over 3,500 alumni in 130 countries.

"The Anatomy of a Large-Scale Hypertextual Web Search Engine." By Sergey Brin and Lawrence Page. Computer Science Department, Stanford University, CA. http://infolab.stanford.edu/~backrub/google.html

Resources – Microsoft

Wikipedia – Microsoft

Microsoft https://en.wikipedia.org/wiki/Microsoft

William Henry Gates IIII (Bill Gates) https://en.wikipedia.org/wiki/Bill_Gates

Mary Maxwell Gates https://en.wikipedia.org/wiki/Mary_Maxwell_Gates

Bill Gates Sr. https://en.wikipedia.org/wiki/Bill_Gates_Sr.

Melinda French Gates https://en.wikipedia.org/wiki/Melinda_French_Gates

Bill and Melinda Gates Foundation
https://en.wikipedia.org/wiki/Bill_%26_Melinda_Gates_Foundation

Paul Allen https://en.wikipedia.org/wiki/Paul_Allen

Warren Buffett https://en.wikipedia.org/wiki/Warren_Buffett

Satya Nadella https://en.wikipedia.org/wiki/Satya_Nadella

Bill Gates 'house https://en.wikipedia.org/wiki/Bill_Gates%27s_house

The Giving Pledge https://en.wikipedia.org/wiki/The_Giving_Pledge

Microsoft Bing [Search Engine]
https://en.wikipedia.org/wiki/Microsoft_Bing

Cascade Investment, LLC
https://en.wikipedia.org/wiki/Cascade_Investment

Microsoft Teams https://en.wikipedia.org/wiki/Microsoft_Teams

Philanthrocapitalism https://en.wikipedia.org/wiki/Philanthrocapitalism

Inside Bill's Brain: Decoding Bill Gates.
https://en.wikipedia.org/wiki/Inside_Bill's_Brain:_Decoding_ Bill_Gates

David Boies https://en.wikipedia.org/wiki/David_Boies

Robert F. Kennedy https://en.wikipedia.org/wiki/Robert_F._Kennedy_Jr.

Newspapers Articles – Microsoft

Calfas, Jennifer. "Bill Gates Calls Jeffrey Epstein Meeting a Mistake." Wall Street Journal. August 5, 2021.

Cooper, Anderson. "Bill Gates opens up about his divorce and Jeffrey Epstein." CNN. August 5, 2021.

Das, Anupreeta and Karmin, Craig. "This Man's Job: Make Bill Gates Richer." Wall Street Journal. September 19, 2014.

Duffy, Clare. "Bill Gates was told to stop 'inappropriate' emails with Microsoft employee in 2008, report says". CNN Business. October 19, 2021.

Flitter, Emily and Stewart, James B. "Bill Gates Met With Jeffrey Epstein Many Times, Despite His Past." New York Times. October 18, 2021.

Francis, Theo. "Bill Gates Transfers $850 Million in Deere Shares to Melinda French Gates." Wall Street Journal. May 18, 2021.

Glazer, Emily. "Microsoft Executives Told Bill Gates to Stop Emailing a Female Staffer Years Ago." Wall Street Journal. October 18, 2021.

Glazer, Emily and Safdar, Khadeeja." Melinda Gates Was Meeting With Divorce Lawyers Since 2019 to End Marriage With Bill Gates." Wall Street Journal. May 9, 2021.

Glazer, Emily, Baer, Justin, and Safdar, Khadeeja. "Warren Buffett to Quit as Gates Foundation Trustee." Wall Street Journal. June 23, 2021.

Glazer, Emily, Baer Justin, Safdar, Khadeeja and Tilley, Aaron. "Bill Gates Left Microsoft Board Amid Probe Into Prior Relationship With Staffer." Wall Street Journal. May 16, 2021.

Goldman, Maya. "Gates Foundation Gift to Support Covid-19 Testing at Historically Black Colleges." Wall Street Journal. October 13, 2020.

Jurgensen, John. "In Bill Gates's Mind, a Life of Processing." Wall Street Journal. September 19, 2019.

Kessler, Sarah. "The Week in Business: Conglomerates Break Up." New York Times. November 14, 2021.

Kristof, Nicholas D. "For Third World, Water Is Still a Deadly Drink." New York Times. January 9, 1997.

Macleod, Alan. "Conflict of Interest? Bill Gates Gave $319 Million to Major Media Outlets, Documents Reveal." Montpress News. November 17, 2021.

McKay Betsey. "Bill Gates Has Regrets." Wall Street Journal. May 11, 2020.

McKay, Betsey and Glazer, Emily. "Gates Foundation Reveals Plan in Case Co-Chairs Can't Work Together." Wall Street Journal. July 7, 2021.

Pacheco, Inti, Cole, Dave and Francis, Theo. "Photos: Inside Bill Gate's Net Worth. There's More Than Microsoft." Wall Street Journal. August 21, 2021.

Ziobro, Paul. "Bill and Melinda Gates to Divorce After 27 Years." Wall Street Journal. May 4, 2021.

Websites – Microsoft

Bill and Melinda Gates Foundation, Melinda French Gates, Co-Chair and Trustee.

Gates Notes, The Blog of Bill Gates.

Paul Allen

Pivotal Ventures, A Melinda French Gates Company, founded in 2015.

The Giving Pledge, founded by Bill and Melinda Gates and Warren Buffett in 2009.

YouTube – Microsoft

Bill Gates: "But Epstein Is Dead!". The Beau Show. October 26, 2021.

Communication Professor Reacts to Bill Gates Interview on PBS. Communication Coach Alex Lyon. October 5, 2021.

Bill Gates - Microsoft Antitrust Deposition - Highlights. United States v. Microsoft Corp. August 28, 1998.

Live Streaming TV Shows – Microsoft

Inside Bill's Brain: Decoding Bill Gates. a three-part documentary streaming television series created and directed by Davis Guggenheim. The series explores the mind and motivations of Bill Gates, co-founder and former CEO of Microsoft and founder of the Bill and Melinda Gates Foundation, together with his then-wife. Distributor: Netflix. Original Release Date: September 20, 2019.

Books – Microsoft

Bishop, Matthew and Green, Michael. Philanthrocapitalism: How Giving Can Save the World. Kindle Edition. Bloomsbury Press. June 1, 2010.

Gladwell, Malcolm. The Tipping Point: How Little Things Can Make a Big Difference. Kindle Edition. Little, Brown and Company. November 1, 2006.

Kennedy, Robert F. Jr. The Real Anthony Fauci: Bill Gates, Big Pharma, and the Global War on Democracy and Public Health. Audible Audiobook. Bruce Wagner (Narrator), Skyhorse Publishing, Inc. November 16, 2021.

McGregor, JR. Business Biographies and Memoirs: 6 Manuscripts: Jeff Bezos, Elon Musk, Steve Jobs, Bill Gates, Jack Ma, Richard Branson. Kindle Edition. CAC Publishing LLC. September 26, 2018.

Characters |

Real and Imagined

Imagined Characters

Imagined characters are being made redundant, replaced by AI Robots (Artificial Intelligence Robots). These characters are middlemen, with no authority or power to understand or solve problems. Most humans in these positions hate their jobs and are quitting in droves, moving on to greener pastures.

Jacky Jack Ass | Customer Care Representative

Silly Sales | Social Media has Made Silly Sales Obsolete

Minus Marketing | No Need for Traditional Marketing

Looney Lawyer | The Loner Legal Beagle

Arnold Accountant | Poor Arnold Has Been Replaced

Real Characters – Amazon

Jeff Bezos, née Jeffrey Preston Jorgensen | Founder of Amazon Businessman, media proprietor, investor, computer engineer

MacKenzie Scott, née Tuttle, formerly Bezos | Co-founder of Amazon | Novelist, philanthropist

Andy Jassy | CEO of Amazon July 5, 2021 | Amazon lifer

Preston Bezos | Oldest son of Jeff Bezos and MacKenzie Scott

Lauren Sánchez | News Anchor, media personality and Jeff Bezos' girlfriend

Dan Jewett | Science Teacher and MacKenzie Scott's second husband

Toni Morrison (deceased) | Princeton professor, novelist, essayist, children's book writer

Real Characters – Apple

Steven Paul Jobs, née Abdul Lateef Jandali, (deceased October 5, 2011) | Co-Founder - Apple, Investor - Pixar, Founder - NeXt.

Laurene Powell Jobs, Steve Job's widow and mother of three Jobs children

Reed Paul Jobs | Cancer Researcher, Emerson Collective |Eldest child and only son of Steve and Laurene, born 1991

Erin Sienna Jobs | Architect and Designer | Middle child and eldest daughter of Steve and Laurene, born 1995.

Eve | Equestrian | Youngest daughter of Steve and Laurene, born 1998.

Joseph Campbell (deceased), He gained recognition in Hollywood when George Lucas credited Campbell's work as influencing his Star Wars saga.

Patrick Takaya Solomon, producer and director of Finding Joe, a film about the hero's journey.

Joanna Hoffman, 1981 and 1982 Winner of the I Stood Up to Steve Jobs Award.

Debi Coleman, 1983 Winner of the I Stood Up To Steve Jobs Award.

Samuel L. Hayes, Professor of Investment Banking and Corporate Finance Executive Education Program Director at the Harvard Business School (1980)

Dan Bricklin, Co-Creator of VisiCalc, A Problem That Changed The World | Dan Bricklin | TEDxBeaconStreet

Pete Musser, née Warren Van Dyke Musser, | Co-Founder with fellow Leigh University alumni, Vincent G. "Buck" Bell of Safeguard Scientifics

Joe Stango, Tek Medics LLC, Stuart, Florida

Craig Schramm, Schramm Physical Therapy, Inc. Stuart, Florida

Real Characters – Facebook

Mark Zuckerberg (Zuck) | Internet entrepreneur, Philanthropist, Media Proprietor

Pricilla Chan | Pediatrician, Philanthropist | Cofounder and co-CEO of Chan Zuckerberg Initiative
https://en.wikipedia.org/wiki/Priscilla_Chan

Maxima Chan Zuckerberg (Max) | first daughter of Priscilla Chan and Mark Zuckerberg

August Chan Zuckerberg | second daughter of Priscilla Chan and Mark Zuckerberg

Sheryl Sandberg | COO Facebook, former VP Global Online Sales and Operations at Google.

Ken Burns | Filmmaker

Jessica Su | Roblox, formerly Facebook

Real Characters – Google

Sergey Mikhaylovich Brin, born August 21, 1973, Moscow, Russian SFSR, Soviet Union (now Russia) Citizenship United States (since 1979), Soviet Union (1973-1979)

Larry Edward Page, born March 26, 1973, Lansing, Michigan. Co-Founder of Google and Alphabet Inc. , Co-Creator of PageRank. Computer scientist, Internet engineer. Spouse Lucinda Southworth (m.2007). 2 children.

Anne Wojcicki, (born July 23, 1973), Palo Alto, California. Co-Founder and CEO of 23andMe. Former Spouse of Sergey Brin (m. 2007; d.2015). Parents: Esther Wojcicki and Stanley Wojcicki. Sister Susan Wojcicki. 2 children

Susan Diane Wojcicki, (born July 5, 1968), Santa Clara, California. CEO of YouTube. Parents: Esther Wojcicki and Stanley Wojcicki. Sister Anne Wojcicki. Spouse Don Troper (m.1998). 5 children.

Sundar Pichai. (Born June 10, 1972), India. CEO of Alphabet and Google.

Sheryl Sandberg, a bit player at Google, number two at Facebook.

Zach Vorhies, Google whistleblower.

Real Characters – Microsoft

Bill Gates nee William Henry Gates III. b. October 8, 1965. Harvard University (dropped out). Occupation: software developer - investor - entrepreneur. Co-founder, Bill and Melinda Gates Foundation; Chairman and founder, Branded Entertainment Network; Chairman and founder, Cascade Investments; Chairman and founder, TerraPower; Founder, Breakthrough Energy

Technology advisor of Microsoft. Former Board Member, Berkshire Hathaway and Microsoft.

Mary Maxwell Gates nee Mary Ann Maxwell. b. July 5, 1929, d. June 10, 1994. University of Washington (BA). Occupation: School teacher, businesswoman. Spouse: Bill Gates Sr. (m. 1951). Children 3, including Bill.

Bill Gates Sr. nee William Henry Gates III. b. November 30, 1925, d. September 14, 2020. Occupation: lawyer, philanthropist. Spouses: Mary Maxwell (m. 1951, died 1994); Mimi Gardner (m. 1996).

Melinda French Gates nee Melinda Ann Gates, b. August 15, 1964. Duke University (BA, MBA). Occupation: Co-Chair and Founder, Bill and Melinda Gates Foundation. Spouse: Bill Gates (m. 1995, div. 2021). Children: 3 (Jenn, Rory, Phoebe).

Paul Allen nee Paul Gardner Allen, b. January 1, 1953, d. October 15, 2018. Washington State University (dropped out). Occupation: Co-founder, Microsoft; Chairman and co-founder, Vulcan Inc.; Owner, Seattle Seahawks and Portland Trail Blazers; Part-owner of Seattle Sounders; Founder, Allen Institute for Brain Science; Founder, Allen Institute for Cell Science; Founder, Allen Institute for Artificial Intelligence; Founder, Apex Learning; Founder, Stratolaunch Systems; Co-founder, Mojave Aerospace Ventures; .Strategy advisor of Microsoft. Sister, Judy Allen.

Steve Ballmer nee Steven Anthony Ballmer, b. March 24, 1965, Detroit, Michigan. Harvard University (BA), Stanford (MBA dropout). Occupation: Investor and businessman; Former CEO, Microsoft. Spouse: Connie Snyder (m. 1990), children 3.

Warren Buffet nee Warren Edward Buffet, b. August 30, 1930, Omaha, Nebraska. University of Pennsylvania Wharton School, University of Nebraska-Lincoln (BS), Columbia University (MS). Occupation: Businessman, investor, philanthropist; Leadership - Berkshire Hathaway with Charles Munger. Spouses: Susan Thompson (m. 1952, died 2004); Astrid Marks (m. 2006). Children 3, Susan Alice Buffet, Howard Graham Buffet, Peter Buffet.

Satya Nadella nee Satya Narayana Nadella, b. August 19, 1967, Pharma-funded mainstream media has convinced millions of Americans that Dr. Anthony Fauci is a hero. He is anything but.

As director of the National Institute of Allergy and Infectious Diseases (NIAID), Dr. Anthony Fauci dispenses $6.1 billion in annual taxpayer-provided funding for scientific research, allowing him to dictate the subject, content, and outcome of scientific health research across the globe. Fauci uses the financial clout at his disposal to wield extraordinary influence over hospitals, universities, journals, and thousands of influential doctors and scientists - whose careers and institutions he has the power to ruin, advance, or reward.

During more than a year of painstaking and meticulous research, Robert F. Kennedy Jr. unearthed a shocking story that obliterates media spin on Dr. Fauci...and that will alarm every American - Democrat or Republican - who cares about democracy, our Constitution, and the future of our children's health.

The Real Anthony Fauci reveals how "America's Doctor" launched his career during the early AIDS crisis by partnering with pharmaceutical companies to sabotage safe and effective off-patent therapeutic treatments for AIDS. Fauci orchestrated fraudulent studies and then pressured US Food and Drug Administration (FDA) regulators into approving a deadly chemotherapy treatment he had good reason to know was worthless against AIDS. Fauci repeatedly violated federal laws to allow his Pharma partners to use impoverished and dark-skinned children as lab rats in deadly experiments with toxic AIDS and cancer chemotherapies.

In early 2000, Fauci shook hands with Bill Gates in the library of Gates '$147 million Seattle mansion, cementing a partnership that would aim to control an increasingly profitable $60 billion global vaccine enterprise with unlimited growth potential. Through funding leverage and carefully cultivated personal relationships with heads of state and leading media and social media institutions, the Pharma-Fauci-Gates alliance exercises dominion over global health policy.

The Real Anthony Fauci details how Fauci, Gates, and their cohorts use their control of media outlets, scientific journals, key government and quasi-governmental agencies, global intelligence agencies, and influential scientists and physicians to flood the public with fearful propaganda about COVID-19 virulence and pathogenesis, and to muzzle debate and ruthlessly censor dissent.

Acknowledgements

Complexity = Corruption

Credit for the title of this series goes to Fareed Zakaria GPS (Global Public Square). The Time article in 2011 caught my attention when I was an MBA Student at Bainbridge Graduate Institute. The article is about the Complexity of the US Tax Code, which Zakaria says:

> "The U.S. tax system is not simply corrupt; it is corrupt in a deceptive manner that has degraded the entire system of American government."
>
> Complexity Equals Corruption, Fareed Zakaria, Time Magazine, Oct. 31, 2011

Complexity = Corruption can be applied to Big Tech, Big Pharma, Big Non-Profit, and to any organization that equates Global and Scale with success. In my opinion, success is serving one's community well.

Individuals and Organizations

I am writing this series based on my experiences - some good learning, some not so much. My opinions are my own, feel free to disagree privately, and respect that I have a right to my opinions.

I have lived a charmed life, meeting folks from all over the world and all walks of life. I will use real first names for folks in my stories. If my experiences was negative I will make up an alias, unless said person/organization asks me to use their real name.

I will identify public figures (Elected Officials, Public Servants, Attorneys, Accountants, etc.) by their full name and position, if appropriate.

In Gratitude

To Patti Lucia, Teacher and friend of many years. Patti encouraged me to write about my life experiences in the context of politics of place and kept me on task.

To my cousin Ron Panton and his widow, Lynne, for their care and concern in navigating life.

To Mariah Fenton Gladis, Gestalt psychotherapist, who taught me to stand tall and never give up.

To Patti Messina, trauma (PTSD) therapist, for helping me unlock my mind and put pen to paper as an activist author.

To Kali Browne, for her patience and caring in teaching me what it means to be a self-published author.

To Ashe Rodrigues, for her insightful cover design

To all the folk I met along the way who have shared stories which informed my work.

Write A Letter

A handwritten envelope with a return address and an Artist inspired USPS stamp is hard to ignore. USPS Stamps can be purchased at https://store.usps.com/store/home.

Write a separate letter for each problem. The Person responding to your letter is only empowered to pay $100.00 on a general complaint. Cutting corners may save you time and cost you money.

Address your letter to Office of the President/ CEO, put your letter, which can be hand written or typed but hand signed, in a hand written envelope, with an original USPS stamp and mail.

If your letter is to Amazon…

Jeff Bezos, Executive Chairman
Andy Jassy, CEO
Amazon dot com, Inc.
410 Terry Avenue North
Seattle, WA 98109-5210

Suggested wording….

I **Love** Amazon most of the time, but sometimes have this problem.

My suggested solution to my problem is….

Enclosed is my invoice for $100.00 or 10 times the cost of the defective item I received from Amazon.

Respectfully submitted,

Your Name

Amazon Customer

Coming Soon

As an activist author, I write about **Politics of Place**, five e-books to a series, which make it easy for me and my readers to remember.

2022 is going to be a watershed year for me and my work as an activist author.

On Monday January 17, 2022, the anniversary of Martin Luther King, Jr.'s birthday, I will unveil the story of Chuck Rogers, Navy Seal (retired) and my breakfast buddy at Aunt D's Diner on the medical mile in Stuart, Florida.

The media announcement event will be at American Legion Post 126 in Jensen, featuring Chuck Rogers (Navy Seal retired) and Vietnam Vet and his hareem - the Auxiliary of American Legion Post 126.

My next **Politics of Place** - series of 5 - will focus on the Surfside Condo Tragedy and my experiences in Florida.

1. The Vinoy Park Hotel and St. Petersburg Beach
2. Fisher Island
3. Surfside Condo Tragedy
4. 2180 Lake Osborne Dive
5. Living on the Medical Mile in Stuart Florida

Stay tuned - I promise a wild ride.

Author's Bio

I have been seated at the table – rather, more accurately, been seated behind the white men seated at the table and told to hold my tongue – at the launch of some of the most radical new business models of the last century.

I have had a front row seat for every new finance and/or economic theory that came down the pike.

This is a dubious honor. I have watched these same new business models crash and burn, take jobs, destroy families, make ghost towns of cities, compromise our health and well-being, and rob us of our happiness. With the economic meltdown of 2008, I watched as my retirement fund plummeted 42% percent from the top of the market in 2007 to the bottom in 2009.

My life has been magical. I have over 70 years life/work experience and an excellent educational background.

Syracuse University (1965) – In my Accounting courses, I learned to fill in forms and play games with numbers. In Anthropology and Public Speaking, I learned storytelling and gained an appreciation of other cultures.

Harvard Business School – Corporate Finance Executive Education (1982) – I learned about OPM (Other People's Money), the strategy that brought the Global Financial Markets to their knees in 2008.

University of Pennsylvania – Organizational Dynamics (1999) – I learned that student's work is only valued when it follows a structured academic path. My Master's thesis, **A New Model for the Creative Use of College Endowments to Reduce College Tuition** would have prevented today's student loan crisis. Penn had no mechanism for "the administrators" to listen to students.

Bainbridge Graduate Institute (BGI) (2013) – I learned the importance of social media to listening deeply and delivering my message.

At an early age, I learned to communicate by listening. At my current age, I feel driven to share the knowledge and understanding amassed during my lifetime. Now I am speaking out.

—Diane Freaney, The Cat Lady